Mr. Nate Berkus

THE
THINGS
THAT
MATTER

NATE
BERKUS

PHOTOGRAPHY BY ROGER DAVIES

SPIEGEL & GRAU | NEW YORK

Published in the United States by Spiegel & Grau,
an imprint of The Random House Publishing Group,
a division of Random House, Inc., New York.

SPIEGEL & GRAU and Design is a registered trademark
of Random House, Inc.

Library of Congress Cataloging-in-Publication Data

Berkus, Nate
The things that matter / Nate Berkus.
p. cm.
ISBN 978-0-679-64431-6
eBook ISBN 978-0-679-64432-3
1. Berkus, Nate—Themes, motives.   2. Interior decoration—
Psychological aspects.   I. Title.
NK2004.3B47 A4 2012
747.092—dc23   2012032445

Printed in the United States of America on acid-free paper

www.spiegelandgrau.com

987654321

FIRST EDITION

Photography by Roger Davies

Additional photography by Rainer Hosch and Kevin Trageser

Book design by Gabriele Wilson Design

TO F.

I've always believed your home should tell *your* story. That pine table over there? I found it in a shop just outside of Mexico City. The sun was beating down and I was a little hungry, but I saw it and I knew I wanted to look at it every day. Those cuff links? They belonged to somebody I loved; we picked them out on one of the most perfect days we ever spent together. That tortoise shell on the wall? There was one exactly like it in my mother's house and I can't see it without thinking about a thousand inedible family dinners. Each object tells a story and each story connects us to one another and to the world. The truth is, things matter. They have to. They're what we live with and touch each and every day. They represent what we've seen, who we've loved, and where we hope to go next. They remind us of the good times and the rough patches, and everything in between that's made us who we are.

—NATE

CONTENTS

THE
THINGS
THAT
MATTER

OVER THE YEARS I'VE READ LOTS OF stories about people who knew exactly who and what they were going to be by the time they were done teething. In fact, I envy anybody who can make their way through childhood and adolescence with that level of confidence. In any case, it did become clear early on that I was a creative person, but when you're a kid growing up in suburban Minneapolis, it's hard to imagine that you'll be starting your own design firm at the age of 22, let alone joining the Oprah Winfrey team, flying all over the country doing makeovers, writing books, producing films, hosting your own TV show, and developing a home design collection that's accessible to everyone. I don't know where you were in junior high, but I was way too busy praying for clear skin and debating whether Madonna was really better than Cyndi Lauper to worry about the big picture.

I did know I felt out of place, and restless, and adventurous in a way that some of my friends did not, and I knew there were things I wanted to see and do and experience in my life that most of the people around me could take or leave. I always sort of sensed there

was a wider world out there—something beyond just taking the bus to and from Hebrew school.

I may have resisted acknowledging it throughout my teenage years, but I now understand that the joy I take in transforming interiors comes from my mom, an interior designer, who has always been about creating a beautiful home. Rooms in our house were in perpetual motion. Fabric samples were laid out everywhere. Overnight a storeroom would become a spare bedroom; a spare bedroom, a TV watching den; a den, a spot for wrapping presents. If my mother wanted to hang a huge canvas in the living room, but couldn't find a painting she could afford, or one she loved enough, she would just paint something herself.

My mother had, and has to this day, an unbelievable sense of scale. She's an artist who is amazingly skilled at laying out a space. Not only are her rooms comfortable; they make perfect sense. Thanks to her, my earliest memories center around design, collecting, and figuring out where everything should go. While other kids were studying algebra, I was studying my mom's collection of tortoise glass. Instead of watching *The Love Boat,* I was watching as she pounded hooks into the living room wall, or helping to stuff a newly reupholstered chair into the trunk of her car.

But it wasn't only my mother. For my dad, an entrepreneur and businessman, everything had to be the best, the finest, the top of the line. His shirts and suits back in the 1980s were all custom-made and immaculately tailored. His shoes were Italian, his cars were hot. As a founder of the National Sports Collectors

Convention, he was able to bring his business sense in line with his collector's mentality, a nostalgist's love for old, high-quality things. I remember him saying to me, "You have to dress well in this world, because everyone notices what you're wearing and they make a decision about you immediately. And anything you say after that, well, if they're smart, people will listen, even if they've already sized you up—but Nate, most people are not that smart."

With parents like these, it was hard not to absorb a love of design, harmony, precision, quality, and beauty. Their lessons lasted—their marriage did not.

My parents split up when I was 2 years old. We were living in Los Angeles at the time, and after the divorce, my mother and I returned to Minnesota, where her parents lived, and where she eventually met and married my stepfather. Throughout my childhood, I would fly back to California to visit my dad. I was what the airlines called an "unaccompanied minor." Over time I developed such precocious assurance that when the flight crew told me they could release me only to a parent or guardian, I would answer with all the breeziness of a 6-year-old kid, "It's okay, my father is meeting me downstairs. I know what to do." And then I'd go down the escalator, find my suitcase on the carousel, head outside the terminal, flag down my dad (or the driver he'd sometimes send), and that was all there was to it. Today, when I tell this to friends with young children, their jaws drop and they all say how fortunate I am that my face never graced the side of a milk carton. But hopping on a plane to see my father was the only thing I'd ever really known and it felt perfectly natural to me. I was a capable kid and I think the experience taught me to navigate the world with a degree of independence and flexibility and fearlessness that still serves me well.

Back home in Minnesota, though, I was a boy with one dream and one dream only: I wanted—no, strike that, I was *desperate* for—a room of my own. You see, in those days I shared a room with my little brother, Jesse, and it wasn't pretty. He was the Oscar to my Felix: messy, careless, and just a little bit sticky— exactly the way a kindergartner is supposed to be. I, on the other hand, was a triple Virgo: frighteningly organized and utterly meticulous—exactly the way a controlling 5th-grade neat freak is supposed to be. I wanted the laundry stacked, sorted, and put away the second it came out of the dryer, whereas my brother lived happily with stuff tossed all over the place. The only LEGO-free zone I was able to maintain was my bed, and believe me, I made it flawlessly. Even as a 10-year-old, I remember trying to explain to my mother and stepfather how upset and frustrated a messy room made me. But they just couldn't grasp it.

*Mom and Dad,
California, 1970*

They wanted me to be playing with baseballs and frogs while I wanted to be scouring garage sales.

I don't know if my mother simply got fed up with refereeing the epic battles between Jesse and me or if it was starting to dawn on her that I just wasn't a baseball-and-frog kind of guy, which is what I'd told her when she signed me up for T-ball. Actually, I believe the exact quote was, "I don't like direct sunlight, I don't like the feeling of grass under my feet, and I don't like mosquitos, so I don't know why you think I'm going to enjoy a summer of this!" But my parents more than made up for it in the fall, giving me the greatest present I could've ever imagined for my 13th birthday. Forget the savings bonds, fountain pens, and Kiddush cup that most Bar Mitzvah boys receive, my mother and stepfather announced that they would be allowing me to renovate an unfinished section of the basement—concrete floors and no drywall—and turn it into my own bedroom.

Moving into a space that I could call mine and, even better, watching it gradually take shape was a major turning point for me. I was involved in every single design decision. The rest of our house may have been done in French Country, but my bedroom was going to be grays, blacks, and reds—a subterranean oasis of the urban '80s in the dead-center of suburban Minnesota. During class, I sat staring at the clock, waiting for the afternoon bell to ring. Most kids race home to play video games or kick a soccer ball; I ran all the way from the bus stop to see if my countertops had come in, or if the guys had installed the bathroom sink yet. In a matter of months, my bedroom had gray carpet with darker gray pin dots, built-in oak furniture with satin-nickel pulls, gray laminate countertops, pale gray grass-cloth wall covering, and a gray laminate bed with red-and-white bedding. The bathroom was white tile, with gray countertops and oak cabinets with a clear stain. You know, just your basic 13-year-old kid's space circa 1984.

Mom and me,
Minneapolis Airport
on the way to
boarding school

Without having this design laboratory of my own, I seriously doubt I would ever have had the confidence so many years later to make sweeping design decisions (let alone have other people foot the bill for them). Over the next few years, I must have rearranged that room a thousand times. Some kids spent their allowance going to see *Indiana Jones and the Temple of Doom;* I spent mine on a great-looking lamp I'd found at the flea market and a ceramic bowl from a neighborhood garage sale. Friends who came for sleepovers had no idea what they were in for. I would get a thought in my head about where I wanted my bed to go or I'd become fixated on gluing something to the ceiling, and we'd get to work—sometimes for hours.

I couldn't leave that bedroom alone. I reorganized. I reinterpreted. I reframed. I had three bookshelves and my idea of a really good time was to remove all the dust covers from my books, then put them back on, just to see how they looked. Even more thrilling, my bedroom connected to the small storage room where my stepfather kept his tools. I'd get an idea, like, maybe, hanging a canopy over my bed, and before you could say "popcorn ceiling," I'd be up on a stepladder with a sheet, a staple gun, and a pocketful of thumbtacks. The vast majority of my teen years was spent trying to make that sheet hang from the ceiling, all the while thinking, *There's got to be a way to do this.* Just as I would do sixteen years later on *The Oprah Winfrey Show*, I'd prepare my own "reveal" moments, dragging my barely patient mother into the basement and flinging open the door to show how new and improved the place looked with the bed in this corner and the bookshelves in that corner. Sometimes she was kind enough to shriek, "Oh my God!" but as a designer, she also had the wherewithal to call a spade a spade and say, "That doesn't work for me at all."

Jesse, Marni, and me
Dan, Steve, and Bob

Does this sound a little odd to you? I guess maybe it was. But back in the early 1980s, I didn't know anybody who wasn't kind of quirky. Wham! and The Cure were in. So was androgyny and eyeliner. Our city was the mall, transportation was a skateboard plastered in neon stickers, the accessories of choice were fluorescent rubber bracelets worn a dozen at a time. My friend Ronnie was obsessed with collecting watches. Another friend lived for GUESS jeans and carving his hair into a mohawk. Some turned *Synchronicity* T-shirts into their daily uniform, while others devoted their every waking moment to following the Minnesota Vikings pre-season. My obsession was that 14 x 14 room in our basement—the one part of my life that could actually look the way I decided it should look, the one place that could change and grow and reveal and conceal, according to my mood. It was where I could most be myself as I attempted to figure out who exactly that was. And though I couldn't have put it into words at the age of 13, playing around with stuff and receiving a concrete visual reward at the end is a big part of what design has always been for me.

The stuff I loved playing with then is the stuff I still love to play with, and it came from prowling flea markets and yard sales and auctions and antique shops in the little communities surrounding my hometown. My mother watched me save my allowance and spend it on the things that mattered to me, listening to me

THE STUFF I LOVED PLAYING WITH THEN IS THE STUFF I STILL LOVE TO PLAY WITH.

say over and over again, "I really want that for my room," as I stood there waiting for the person in the antiques place to return with the key that opened the cabinet that held whatever treasure I was lusting after. What can I say? I'm a sucker for the hunt, that eureka moment when you find something amazing at a good price that can potentially transform the entire spirit of a room. The more overstuffed and overloaded and junky and trinket-filled a shop was, the more my heart started pounding, and that feeling hasn't quit or grown old since 7th grade.

My design (and real-life) world expanded when I turned 17 and my parents sent me to boarding school in Massachusetts. They were worried I was heading down the wrong path, and thought that a change of scenery might be useful. Like many small communities, our suburb could be neatly divided into two parts, with

the upper-middle-class Jewish families on one side, and the bowling alleys and fast food chains on the other. I frequently gravitated to the other side of town, which was a fantastic breeding ground for antiques stores and pawnshops.

Most of my friends got cars when they turned 16 and used those cars to go to parties where we'd drink beer and listen to music turned up way too loud and smoke pot. It was the '80s and it was the suburbs and there really wasn't much else to do. But it turns out that you can spend only so much time watching your buddy wash his Mustang before you start feeling like you're trapped in a John Hughes movie. The truth is, I was bored out of my mind.

I was also in debt. The department store where I worked after school gave me a store credit card, but neglected to give me a lecture on restraint, so like any 9th grader worth his salt, I immediately began charging everything credit could buy, which included a big chunk of the men's department. On top of that, I was using my stepfather's gas card not just to fill up my own car, but the cars of all my friends. Unleaded gas, on the house! "Why does Nate have to have that fancy watch?" my stepfather would ask. "Why does he have to wear those expensive shoes?" He thought my value system was way out of whack, and you know something? He was absolutely right.

Boarding school may be considered home-away-from-home-for-the-maladjusted in some circles, but I genuinely loved the entire experience. Plus, my mother's family was from the East Coast, and being at Cushing Academy gave me a chance to explore that part of the world. At first I didn't get it. Why did everyone dress in such an expensively sloppy way? Why did the school make us wear a coat and tie for dinner one day a week? What was the architecture all about? How come nothing looked shiny and new? Why did my cousins, who lived

Cushing Academy, Ashburnham, Massachusetts, 1990

9

in a leafy suburb outside of Boston, have those old plates out on display? What was with all the needlepoint pillows and the American antiques? And the real question: What was wrong with me that I showed up on campus with gel in my hair, only to be greeted by a student body outfitted head-to-toe in L.L. Bean? Within a week, you couldn't tell me apart from them. (I still think of that time as my Duck Shoe period.)

At Cushing I fell in love with New England. My favorite times were Fall Free weekends, when I visited classmates who lived in Boston and Cambridge and New York City. And I began my fascination with France, thanks to my glamorous French teacher, Sheryl Storm, who had cool earrings, wore her bangs at a very chic angle, and rocked a designer scarf over her shoulder. Here we were, sitting in a classroom at the base of a mountain in western Massachusetts, but believing that we were in the heart of Paris. Ms. Storm made us feel what it would actually be like to wander into a French bakery and order a croissant and *citron presse*. There's a word she taught us, *debrouiller*, which means "to manage" or "to get by." She said that she didn't want us merely to get by, she wanted to see us go to France and be able to "express our personalities." Years later, I sent her a Louis Vuitton bag, with a note saying how much it reminded me of her, and she sent me back one of the most beautiful letters I've ever received.

Anyway, something about that sensibility must have stuck, because when I began going to Lake Forest College outside of Chicago, I remember an overpowering need for Ralph Lauren sheets on my dorm bed. My mother told me I was being ridiculous but I was so determined, I ended up scoring those sheets on sale at T.J. Maxx. I'll go out on a limb here and venture a guess that I was one of the few freshmen who showed up for school with picture frames and decorative boxes in a hunt theme, too.

When I was a freshman in college I came out to my family and friends. My stepfather was actually the one who first brought the topic up with me. At the start of the summer, it turned out, he'd found a letter from a guy I was dating at the time. But he didn't mention what he'd read until late August, as he was driving me to the airport for the flight back to Chicago. He told me he knew I was gay, but that he was not going to tell my mother—that was up to me. Then he said something that I still think is kind of remarkable. "The reason I didn't talk to you about any of this at the beginning of the summer, Nate," he said, "is because I wanted you to see that the fact I know you're gay would never make me treat you any differently."

He went on to tell me that in many ways, he was relieved. Whatever conflicts he'd observed in me as a kid, whatever had driven me to become who I was, finally made sense to him. "It's been hard for me to be a stepparent to you," he said, "because frankly, I've found it hard to relate to you." My references, my interests, my obsessions, practically none of it made sense to him. And now it did.

I waited until I came home for Thanksgiving two months later to tell my mother. She was extremely supportive. I should add, too, that she was surprised by the news; frankly, I don't think she had ever broken stride long enough to consider if her design-obsessed son might be gay. She told me whoever I was, she loved me regardless, but that she needed to take some time to surrender—and, I imagine, grieve the loss of a fantasy that probably every mother has about her son or daughter. You have to keep in mind that in 1992 the world functioned under a strict don't-ask-don't-tell policy. Marriage, raising children, genuine equality—these concepts weren't even a remote possibility for openly gay men or women. This meant that my mother had to let go of the idea of the life she had always envisioned for me. She was also afraid of telling her own parents, who, as it turned out, were incredibly wonderful and unconditionally loving and, above all, wise when they found out. "You're very lucky," my grandmother said to her. "Don't you see? Nate is telling you this because he wants to keep you in his life."

My father had a harder time. This was a guy who had worked in and around

Steve, me, Dan, Bob, and our father, Bob's wedding, 2004, Newport Beach, California

sports for many years, a world that still doesn't have many gay people in it, at least not many who are open about it. And Orange County, California, where he lived after marrying my stepmother and having three more sons, isn't exactly famous for its liberal Democratic base. "I don't understand," my dad said to me. "You're an attractive guy. You can probably go out with any woman you want. This just makes no sense to me. Why have you done this? Why have you chosen this life?"

"You don't understand," I said. "It wasn't a choice."

For a few years, that was as far as we got. I still saw my father and showed up for family events. I didn't unplug is the point I'm trying to make, but whenever I went to visit, on vacations at the end of the year or in the summer, no one asked any questions about my personal life. My brothers had no idea, either, as my father and stepmother made me promise not to discuss it with them. The tension was tangible. We were reduced to awkward, superficial conversations, until I couldn't take it anymore. It was no reflection on them, I told my dad and stepmother, but I had to tell my brothers, if for no other reason than to explain why whenever they asked me if I was going out with anybody, and if so, whether the woman and I were serious, that, actually, I *was* dating—just not women. My siblings were okay with it, but you have to remember we all came from a fairly sheltered upbringing, and it wasn't until they were older, and got out into the world, where they met other gay people, that it all fell into place for them. Today, I'm happy to say that our whole family is really, really close. And, of course, maybe it goes without saying that not a single one of them will make a serious design decision—or even buy a side table—without first asking me to weigh in.

The topic jelled for my father during a business trip he took to Chicago when I was 26 years old. I'd been running my own design firm for three years. I invited my boyfriend to have dinner with my father and me at a restaurant downtown. It all went okay, but as usual, a lot was left unsaid. I drove my dad to the airport at the end of his trip, and when the flight was delayed, we went across the street to a hotel bar and ordered a couple of drinks.

The conversation was painful at first, but I'd had enough small talk to last a lifetime. My dad let me know that he and my stepmother lived in perpetual fear that someday the phone would ring and the news wouldn't be good—that they'd hear I had done something to myself, hurt myself in some way. "Why would you ever think that?" I asked. "Because," my dad explained, "the life you've chosen for yourself is difficult, and empty, and worrisome, and—"

I looked him in the eye and told him I was going to explain things to him one time, and that I really needed him to hear what I was about to say, and that if, when I was finished, he didn't believe me, that was all right, too. "Do you respect me as your eldest son?" I asked. He did, he told me. "Do you think I'm smart?" He did. "Do you think I'm competent?" He told me he did.

I went on: He knew how I was raised, that we had sat together at the dinner table, that I had absorbed what he'd taught me, that he'd seen up-close how I operated both in the business world and in the world in general, and so far, did he respect what he saw? Yes, he said, he did.

"So, Dad, I'm going to tell you something now, and it is the one thing that will determine whether we have a true relationship or we have next to nothing: I did not choose to be gay," I said. "Why would I choose something that would make my life more difficult? We live in a world that treats homosexuals as second-class citizens, where the laws are stacked against us, where people disapprove of us. Look at me! I didn't choose to be five-eight. If I had any choice in the matter, I would have chosen to be six-one. Let's be honest: *Moses* couldn't part my hair. Do you really think this is the hair I'd have come up with if it were up to me? I find it completely without logic that you believe I have chosen my sexual orientation."

My father sipped his drink for a while, and said at last, "I've never really thought about it that way." Then, "That makes sense. I believe you entirely."

"Okay," I said, "then we're good." And from that moment on, we've continued to be good, to connect.

A few years later, I wrote a chapter for *Crisis*, an anthology devoted to helping teens come out. I tried to drive home the point that as gay people, we carry with us the terrible fear that if we tell the world this single piece of information, that we're gay, no one will love us. What an awful thing to carry around. But I also wanted to make it clear that we have a responsibility to take care of the people we love, because after you share the truth of who you are, they have to go through their own process of accepting this information, and mourning the loss of the life they had envisioned for you.

The life I'd envisioned for myself began taking shape during college, when I spent a year in Paris. If boarding school was one of the first turning points of my life, Paris left corduroys and quadrangles in the dust.

Apart from a few family vacations, if that's how a pontoon boat trip to a Minnesota lake should be categorized (let the record reflect that finding a leech sucking the bottom of your foot is not one of those Kodak moments you want to press in a scrapbook), I did not grow up traveling all over the world. The study

Paris, 1991

THE LIFE I'D ENVISIONED FOR MYSELF BEGAN TAKING SHAPE DURING COLLEGE, WHEN I SPENT A YEAR IN PARIS.

abroad program Lake Forest offered allowed me to spend my junior year in Paris, which was the first time I had ever lived in Europe. I took to France—the people, the spectacular beauty and texture of everyday life, the fact that cheese did not come in individually wrapped slices—as if all this time I were a French expatriate who found himself accidentally coming of age in Minnesota. Along with New York, Mexico City, Rome, and Patmos—a little Greek island in the Aegean Sea that has to be seen to be believed—Paris was and still is one of the few places on this planet where I feel totally at home. In Paris, the history belongs to everyone. It's an incredibly egalitarian city. No matter how much money you have, you can pull up a seat, sip an espresso, and gaze at the Luxembourg Gardens. Partaking in a culture that brought the past into everyday life got under my skin, and has never left me. I found everything about the place fascinating, from the story of the French monarchy to how Paris became world headquarters for luxury goods, to how the French prize a frayed pillow with stuffing coming out of it—they accept things as they are.

At first the pressure of not speaking French was awful. I was interning at a fashion buying office, and my boss insisted that I answer the phones. Whenever I stumbled or said "*le*" instead of "*la*," she would yell at me. When she finally had the decency to fire me, I found an unpaid internship working for a costume jewelry designer, where I set up the showroom and took appointments for American buyers.

I wanted to immerse myself in all things French, but I had so little money, it wasn't always easy. I couldn't afford to eat out. I was literally making pasta in butter on a hot plate in the little room I was renting, with its black armoire, white desk, narrow bed, and assorted trinkets I'd bought from flea markets and street vendors (I went to flea markets religiously every weekend, even if it meant buttered spaghetti 24/7). My sole connection to French culture was my co-worker, Viviane, who despite being ten years older than me was my link to the Parisian nightlife. She took pity on my language skills and empty stomach and would have me to her place for dinner. She introduced me to her friends, people

Me and Viviane,
Paris, 1995

14

who modeled for Jean Paul Gaultier and worked for Yves Saint Laurent, and they all went out of their way to make me feel welcome. I was so broke and so eager to turn into a real Parisian that I decided to sell all my clothes.

The Ralph Lauren flagship store that had just opened in Paris was all the rage. It so happened that I had a full wardrobe of Ralph Lauren stuff that I had lugged overseas with me. Polos, jeans, sweaters, belts—if it had a pony and a mallet on it, I owned it, courtesy of the Minneapolis department store where I'd run up so much debt, and my parents, who knew how much I loved clothes. I came up with a plan: I told my host, whose teenage son was about my size, "I have all these Ralph Lauren clothes that I'm interested in selling. Maybe your friends would like to come over, and we could have a trunk show." Before I knew it, eight Frenchwomen had bought their kids every single piece of clothing I owned. I made 3,000 francs, and for the next eight months my entire wardrobe consisted

of Levi's, T-shirts, a jean jacket, and motorcycle boots. Soon after, the language thing kicked in. I woke up one morning and realized that in my dream I'd been speaking French—and from that day forward, with a few minor changes, I was on a roll *en francais*.

Paris was also the first time I fell in love with someone else's interior. It belonged to my friend Maria, and my favorite room was the cavernous kitchen, complete with a huge old stove, Delft tiles, and an antique oak table on an iron base, surrounded by chairs that didn't match. There were no built-in cabinets, no lazy Susan, nothing even remotely Formica. That kitchen had looked exactly the same for at least a hundred years. I remember thinking, *This room is a real rule-breaker*. It was so unself-conscious in its design that years later when I bought my apartment in Chicago, I think somewhere in the back of my mind I remembered Maria's kitchen and chose to just let the 1950s kitchen be. We all have this knee-jerk reaction, where we start immediately ripping out countertops and updating hardware, but Maria's place was lovely just the way it was and it taught me something about grace and simplicity and the value of a room that's perfectly imperfect. To Maria and her family, that space was just part of ordinary life, the place they sat and had breakfast each morning. But to me, hanging out in that kitchen—where the wine and conversation and laughter had flowed for more than a century—was extraordinary. If I learned to appreciate old things by tagging along behind my mother as she shopped the little vintage stores of Minneapolis, France is where my love of really, *really* old things originated. Paris was also the place where I became completely obsessed with things and their stories—where they came from, where they ended up, how they represent who people are and all that they've loved and seen.

I think people sometimes confuse loving things with being materialistic, or grasping, or lusting after things that tell the world who you are. But to me, surrounding yourself with the things you love has nothing to do with impressing other people or gaining status. Even when I was a kid, I loved the sense of accomplishment I got from finding and bringing home something I loved. What do people's things say about who they are? There's this game I like to play

In my Paris apartment, age 21

with friends and colleagues when we're on a long plane ride. I open up a glossy magazine or one of those SkyMall catalogs in the seatback. Then I turn to the person beside me. "Okay," I say, "if you could pick one thing on this page, what would it be? This ring or that watch? This sofa or that lamp?"

"How come your eyes light up when you look at this particular bed?" I once asked a colleague in the aisle seat next to me, who seemed transfixed by a photo of a bed in a shelter magazine I was paging through. At first she shrugged and said she really had no idea. But a minute or two later, she began telling me all about her great-aunt who smelled like cinnamon and once had a fling with William Powell. "She seemed really stern," my colleague told me as she stared at the picture, "but she used to sneak me lemon drops when my parents weren't looking and she had this fabulously intricate iron bed with lace sheets—you wouldn't figure her for the lace sheet type—and, in a million years, you'd never imagine that she would actually encourage my sister and me to have these massive pillow fights, where we'd all end up laughing until midnight. And when my marriage fell apart," she said quietly, "I crawled home to Indiana and put on a flannel nightgown and got into that old bed and stayed there for weeks, until one day my ancient aunt lobbed a pillow at the side of my head and told me it was time to shave my legs and get back to my life. . . ." And her voice trailed off, momentarily lost in the memory, until a flight attendant interrupted with the offer of a drink. I don't think we've ever mentioned it again, but we don't have to—the connection was made. It turns out that we both know something about feeling alone and depleted and we both understand how to start again from scratch, all thanks to an iron bed in the house of a very smart lady who lived 20 miles south of Bloomington, Indiana.

For me, the most successful interiors in the world are put together by people who surround themselves with objects that bring them joy, and make them feel really at home—a feeling I remember deeply from when I was a 13-year-old kid, finally in a room of his own; a feeling I remember as a boarding school student decorating his cubby hole of a room as the snow fell outside; a feeling I cherish when I think back on my days as a junior boulevardier eating a crepe with powdered sugar I'd bought from a booth on the left bank of Paris; and one I still feel today whenever I look around my New York apartment. As I've said over and over again, our homes should tell the stories of who we are. Not who our decorator is. Not who our friends sometimes think we should be, not who our family occasionally wishes we would be, and not who any number of style magazines tell us we *must* be. At the end of the day, we can't escape who we are

and what we love, and the truth is, it's a mistake even to try. It can take a long time and a lot of soul searching to figure out who we actually are—and to showcase that identity proudly to our friends and family—so when we finally get there, let's live with the stuff that delights and replenishes our senses, the stuff that is filled with the totems and memories that represent the chapters of our life that are written through the things we surround ourselves with.

To that end, I credit my first source of inspiration—namely, my parents, and especially my mother. Oddly enough, for two people who probably sound so similar on paper—she's my mom, I'm her son; she's a decorator, I am, too; we both love estate sales and vintage stuff—we are at polar ends of the design spectrum every time. No exceptions. My mom and I connect around our love of geodes and minerals, but that's about it. Whenever we go to flea markets together, she never, ever reaches for the things I want, and I never, ever reach for the things she wants. "Oh, look—a hand-carved Southwest pony!" she says. "I love that!"

"I know you do," I say. Because, well, I knew she would.

"You don't love it, too, Nate?"

"No," I say, "but I know you do, so I think you should get it."

We do have a few things in common. The kitchen island in my New York apartment, for example, is something she would have in her house (and ten years ago, if you'd told me I would go for it, I would have recommended you be institutionalized). Ditto for the chunky 1950s Mexican pine table that sits in my

FOR ME, THE MOST SUCCESSFUL INTERIORS IN THE WORLD ARE PUT TOGETHER BY PEOPLE WHO SURROUND THEMSELVES WITH OBJECTS THAT BRING THEM JOY.

living room, which I couldn't love more. My 22-year-old self would also be pretty stunned that the 40-year-old me could ever live with a pair of eight-foot-tall saguaro cactuses. Neither would my younger self have understood or have had the confidence for the vintage Native American fabric that covers a pillow on a chair in my living room. My unschooled, untraveled 18-year-old self, who was into classic fabrics like corduroys and cable knit and linen and suede, wouldn't have understood, much less coveted, fabrics and objects from South America or Southeast Asia or Turkey, much less the ceramic pineapple on my side table that my late partner Fernando lugged all the way home from Mexico.

The fact is, over the years we change, we evolve, we discard, we add on, we backtrack, we consolidate, we look at old photos of ourselves and can't believe we were wearing that madras jacket, sporting that awful haircut, working that job. At some point for all of us, people, experiences, and aesthetics come together to create the interiors we live in, the styles we embrace, and the things that we can't live without. As I stand in my home today, I see remnants of that Minnesota boy. I know my style wouldn't be the same without my Midwest upbringing, my California summers, and the people, places, and things I've seen along the way. "Personality," F. Scott Fitzgerald once said, "is an unbroken series of successful gestures." He could have said the exact same thing about the rooms we live in.

I believe that the objects that bring us pleasure and comfort, that make us feel everything's all right in the world, have their origins in the styles and sensibilities we were exposed to growing up. Which is why almost thirty years after they gave an exacting little kid his own basement bedroom to play around in, I owe a giant debt of gratitude to my family, for helping to put me on a path that became my passion.

WHEN I RETURNED TO COLLEGE IN the States from my year in Paris, I landed an internship (with full college credit) at Leslie Hindman Auctioneers in Chicago. Somehow I managed to convince my parents that this internship was more important than attending actual classes, and faster than you can say "But don't college kids belong in a dormitory?" I talked them into pouring whatever money they had set aside for my room and board into a small rental on Huron Street, in the heart of downtown Chicago. After graduating, my plan was to move to Europe, but in a sudden burst of reality, my mother had me call Leslie to find out if she would consider giving me a paid job. Leslie happily told me I could start the following week.

I don't mean to brag but I really managed to distinguish myself as an assistant. The fact is, I have been declared the worst assistant ever to file an invoice. I'm a very mediocre typist, I can't fix a Xerox machine to save my soul, and when you get right down to it, shouldn't grown men and women be capable of getting their own coffee?

LESLIE HINDMAN AUCTIONEERS

215 West Ohio Street
Chicago, Illinois 60610
(312) 670-0010 FAX: (312) 670-4248

December

Dear Friend:

I want to thank all you for your hard work and dedi
1994. It has been one of Leslie Hindman Auctioneer
exciting years ever.

From Rubloff to Napoleon, to the Chicago Stadium
the Auction" and the marathon sales in October an
have pulled together as a team to make this one
successful years since this firm's inception.

Although, many of you are relatively new to our
in which we have grown as a team, and the friendsh
been formed, is remarkable. The energy and enthusiasm eac
of you have brought to every endeavor is greatly appreciated.

I have loved getting to know you, and have delighted in watching
each one of you grow both professionally and personally in the
past 12 months. I have tremendous admiration and respect for all
of you.

I am more excited about the coming year than I have ever been. I
am looking forward to working with you in the coming year to
bring LHA to its next level as a company, as well as maintaining
the professional and lively working atmosphere in which we all
thrive.

Thank you again so much!

I wish you, your family and friends a joyous holiday season and a
wonderful new year!

You are wonderful!!

Love,
Leslie

Nate - you have
tremendous potential -
I'm crazy about you!

The point is, instead of firing me, as the rest of the staff was begging her to do, Leslie summoned me into her office. "I actually think you're smart," she said. "So I am about to make your life really difficult, and we'll see if you can rise to the challenge."

She put me in charge of a series of monthly auctions. My job was to try to convince all the people who were accustomed to buying a new chair for $750 that they were much better off buying a vintage chair from Leslie Hindman Auctioneers for $50. And I wasn't just in charge of handling the auctions, I was also the entire marketing team, the sales force, and while I was at it, the auctioneer, too. "Everyone here is going to hate you," Leslie said, "because you're going to make them work on weekends, and they will find it very hard to believe I gave you this position, but I think you can handle it." Oh, and one more thing: My little monthly auctions had to gross $100,000 a month, she told me, or I was fired.

"Great!" I said, because that's what you say when you're 22 years old and have no clue what you're doing but believe you can do it just the same.

Another of my duties was to set up the showroom every month before the sale. It was during this experience—creating beautiful "rooms" to entice people to bid on the items in them—that I first thought, *Maybe I can actually do this for a living.* It was extraordinary and inspiring for me to see in such an intimate way how other people lived, what they collected, what they inherited, what they bought, what they saved, what they were relieved to walk away from, and what they just couldn't bear to part with. I found all of it fascinating: where they ordered their stationery, why certain people had a home filled with reproductions, while others lived with only antiques. I loved noting trends: China starts mass producing their designs in the 1950s and suddenly chinoiserie begins appearing in upper-middle-class American interiors. And, of course, I loved the personal stories. What could be more interesting than watching an old woman point to a brooch in the jewelry collection that would be putting her grandson through college and hearing her explain that her aunt Eva buried the brooch so the Nazis wouldn't get it. "And after the war," the woman announced triumphantly, "she found it right where she'd left it, under the plum tree in her best friend's yard!" I also got to see my share of tough businessmen suddenly melt. "That was my grandfather's reading chair!" Or "I spent every Friday night sneaking scraps of pot roast to the dog under that mahogany table . . . nobody had the heart to tell my mother how awful her pot roast was!" they'd say, laughing.

It's not enough to know what you're going to sell. A good auctioneer has to know

Me at Leslie Hindman Auctioneers, Chicago, 1995

23

what people are looking to buy. It's really not so different from being a personal shopper; I made a point of always being aware of who was looking for a sideboard for their dining room and who needed a table for their entry. I got to see inside people's homes; I got to know their particular style. And through that job, I met hundreds of people in Chicago, from dealers to real estate developers, many of whom are still my friends. I worked for Leslie Hindman Auctioneers for precisely one year, and thanks to a combination of hustle, youth, and an overwhelming fear of messing up and losing my job, every single month I managed to get that auction house their $100,000.

At the time, I was dating a very successful event planner, and I remember being jealous of his incredible freedom. He worked hard, but if he felt like working out at 10:30 a.m., well, he went to the gym, no questions asked. If he wanted to start his weekend at 2:15 on Friday, he just did it. I, on the other hand, had to wait until 5:01 on Friday afternoon before I could call my life my own again.

We were talking about all of this one day, when he turned to me and said, "Well, why don't you become a decorator? You love decorating, after all."

And in that moment, everything crystallized for me. "You're right," I said. "That would be amazing." Then and there, I decided to form a one-man band. I had business cards made with my name and cell phone number on them. I bought a printer. I set up a small office with a desk and a lamp, and exactly one year later a former co-worker at the auction house came to join me.

Chicago is a city that roots for innovation (think Frank Lloyd Wright and deep-dish pizza), and people who need to catch a break (think the Cubs), so from the beginning, I felt incredibly supported and embraced. The local media was generous to me—my interiors began to get published, and before long I found myself building a client base. It's easy to gloss over the bad days, but the truth is, terms like *liability insurance* and *payroll taxes* are enough to send any new business owner in search of a cold compress and a shot of tequila.

That said, for a long time I couldn't believe clients were really paying me to rummage through vintage stores for remnant fabrics to redo their chairs. It was like earning money to breathe or sleep or eat pasta. Looking back, part of my evolution as a decorator was to let go of what I felt was appropriate, bland, or conventional. When you're getting your feet wet, slowly turning your passion into a business, and gradually growing a reputation, you tend to start off by playing it safe. But as time passed, and I was able to get a little experience under my belt, I began coming into my own, with the emphasis on *my*. *My* vision. *My* aesthetic. And eventually, *my* home.

My pre-computer design notebooks

My first apartment, Chicago, 1995

The first time I saw the Chicago apartment I ended up buying was during the good old days of 10-percent-down mortgages. Even so, the apartment was way too pricey for somebody just starting out. Sheila Starr, my real estate broker, told me about a great place she had in mind for me. But before we visited, she said, there were three things to keep in mind. 1) She was afraid I was going to kill her since the apartment was so much more than I wanted to spend. 2) It was in slightly shabby condition. 3) Despite that, she couldn't live with herself unless she showed it to me.

It was winter, and the place was shadowy. There were no overhead lights, and no lamps, either. The draperies were tattered and there were sun spots on the floor. The apartment had been vacant for many years.

If I was born with any kind of gift, here it is: the ability to walk into any interior and recognize its potential—to know intuitively if the bones are right. And if the bones are weak or broken, to know at once how to reset them so that the interior comes alive. The first thing I noticed about the place, which was built in 1918, was how beautifully crafted everything was. At four thousand square feet, it was truly a grown-up home. The walls were thick. The architecture, redone in the 1950s by Samuel Marx (he designed the New Orleans Museum of Art), was spotless, the master bedroom had fantastic built-in closets, the moldings were simple and perfect. As the rooms unfolded, I began to imagine what it would feel like to live in a space this classic and refined. How I defined myself, how I wanted other people to perceive me—not to mention my passion for vintage hardware and old fireplaces—was right there in front of me, already in place. I knew I'd come home.

Early Nate Berkus
Associates stationery

The one big drawback was the tiny bathroom. Noticing my expression, the broker said, "My friend Bill Blass says that dressing rooms should be large, and—"

I finished the sentence for her. "—bathrooms should be small."

She was silent. "You know, this really *is* your apartment, isn't it?"

I knew there was work to be done. I knew I had to repair and refinish the floors and replace the kitchen linoleum with wood and paint the walls and update the electrical system and install air-conditioning and hunt down screens for all the windows. The apartment would definitely be a project. But the bones were there.

One of the questions people ask me the most is "How can I make this room look good while spending the least amount of money?" That was the question I had to ask myself. I knew buying the place would demolish my savings, and that I was risking pretty much everything. But I've never been afraid of money. It's not because I was born with a trust fund—I wasn't. In my four decades of life, I've had no money, some money, no money again, and lots of money. But I have always, *always* bet on myself. I had to believe I could afford to live in a vintage apartment in a gorgeous old building—and that even if it meant eating nothing but ramen noodles for the rest of my life, I *would own* it.

I still have snapshots from the week I moved in, with my mother's help. "There are four pieces of furniture in a thirty-foot space," she remarked at one point. True enough, but I knew that over time the interior would become a place that spoke to the person I was, and the person I hoped to become. And I have to say, in many ways, I really did come of age in that apartment. It's where I was living when Fernando Bengoechea came into my life.

Fernando and I met in 2003 at a photo shoot for *O at Home* magazine. He had been hired to photograph the makeover process of a living room I was brought in to redo. How many people are lucky enough to have the very first meeting of a great love documented by the nature of what they do professionally? The day I met him, I could see, through his photographs, how he saw me, and I remember thinking, *Things don't get any better than this.*

Fernando was audacious and complicated and spontaneous and sophisticated and charismatic and demanding and graceful and volatile and extravagant and occasionally impossible. And when he walked into the room, he pretty much owned it. He was also contemplative and nurturing and soulful and insightful and intuitive and deeply kind. Our attraction was instantaneous and it was powerful. One week after we began dating, Fernando flew to Chicago to visit me. When he walked into the apartment, I naturally assumed he would be bowled over by

"THE DRESSING ROOMS SHOULD BE LARGE, AND BATHROOMS SHOULD BE SMALL."

Bathroom, Chicago

Closet, Chicago

27

its scale and design, and he was . . . only not quite in the way I imagined. In his typically contrarian style, Fernando said, "You are a more interesting person than this. I'm surprised that you live someplace so traditional."

Fernando always woke up earlier than I did. And after that first night in my apartment, I walked into the living room to find that while I was sleeping, he had rearranged all the furniture. A lot of people would have been hurt or insulted or a bit of both. But I wasn't bothered in the least. I actually kind of *loved* that he'd done that. I loved that as a photographer he was so visual that he couldn't bear to look at something he thought could be improved upon. One reason Fernando was a genius at photographing interiors is that he was just *compelled* to experiment with spaces, to design new rooms and create tableaux that didn't exist. It became a thing with us. We played with our stuff the way some couples do the Sunday *Times* crossword puzzle. I would visit him in New York on the weekends, and we'd spend hours moving his living room around. Though I didn't put it together at the time, we would do the exact same things—reshuffle furniture; swap a picture for a mirror; rearrange books, and surfaces, and closets; add some texture; subtract some pillows, try this higher, that lower—I did in my bedroom as a child. We became partners in the pursuit of creating a feeling of *home*. It was a feeling I had never had so strongly before.

One of the other things Fernando and I had in common was a love of traveling. He had been all over the world, and he was eager for me to see the places he loved most. "You can't really call yourself a sophisticated person if you've only been to Mexico and France," he said. "You have to see the rest of the world." I agreed in theory, but I remember a fight we had early on when during one of my weekend visits to him in New York I urged him to come do a little hunting with me at the 26th Street flea market, which was only a few blocks from where he lived. Nothing I could say would convince him that it wouldn't be filled with junk. He was sure that one of my all-time favorite places in Manhattan would be a ridiculous waste of his time. So I went on my own that morning and I bought a bunch of little things I knew he'd love, including a wonderful French-to-English pocket dictionary from the nineteenth century (it sits on my fireplace mantel today); some handcrafted wooden bowls, rustic yet refined; chunky African beads; and a silver picture frame. I will never forget the look of shock on his face when I handed them to him, one treasure at a time. The man had burned through eight passports in his travels around the world, and I'd just brought him the same stuff he used to jam into his suitcase. "You mean," he said sheepishly, "the entire time I was trying to somehow

Fernando, Italy,

31

fit all these things between my knees on a crowded airplane, they've been sitting on card tables four blocks from my apartment?"

Fernando had taste, much more layered than my own. When I walked into his loft for the first time, I knew in my gut we would end up together. For starters, the place was ridiculously clean. It was bright and light and filled with vintage objects he'd dragged home from Russia and Vietnam, Italy and Thailand, Patagonia and the Basque Country, and a hundred other exotic places from his life on the road. In addition to his sofa on the other side of the room, he had a mattress on the floor in front of the fireplace, draped with a mix of plush, hand-knit blankets in shades of ivory and ecru, across from a wall of books he'd collected from museums and bookshops all over the world. Everywhere my eye landed, I saw something I loved. Each piece had a story to tell. His glazed pottery was from a small village in China; his incense from Esteban in Paris; his pots and pans from South America, so fine they almost made me want to cook (I said *almost*); two floor-to-ceiling shelves were filled with embroidered textiles from Morocco and Mexico and India. The things in his apartment and the stories that went with them opened my eyes to cultures I only dimly knew existed. He made me want to watch the sun come up over the Sea of Galilee and study the tile mosaics of Marrakesh and buy saffron and curry at the Malaysian bazaars. He showed me a bigger life than I'd ever dreamed of for myself.

Fernando rarely went back to the same place twice. There was simply too much else to see. But ten years earlier, while he was working as a photographer's assistant, he'd gone to a small fishing village off the coast of Sri Lanka. He and I were arguing one day about how I never took any real vacations, the kind where

Fernando, Brazil

you unplug from the world for two, maybe even three, weeks. I was trying to build a career, and if somebody needed me, I had to be available, so when he suggested we go somewhere for three entire weeks, he may as well have suggested I bungee jump off the Chrysler Building. "You can make it happen," Fernando pushed. "Where do you want to go?"

You have to pick your battles, and I knew this was a fight I was not going to win. "You decide," I said.

He chose that little fishing village he'd visited a decade before. He booked our flights, and planned out an itinerary. We would land in Bangkok and stay there for two nights. Then we'd go to Cambodia for five nights to see the temples of Angkor, then return to Bangkok for a night, before spending two nights in Sri Lanka, in Colombo. We would visit the tea plantations in Kandy, then spend the rest of our vacation, a little more than a week, on the beach—no ruins to tour, no shops to check out—just being with each other.

On our first day in Bangkok (and my first time ever in Asia), we crossed the river to have breakfast at a small restaurant where the water outside the window came up to our table. You know how every great once in a while you have conversations that stay with you forever, nights when you sit up way too late talking about everything and nothing, days when a short stroll turns into a long walk because the light is beautiful and the words are flowing and nobody wants to stop? We looked out at the water and even though we had already been together a year,

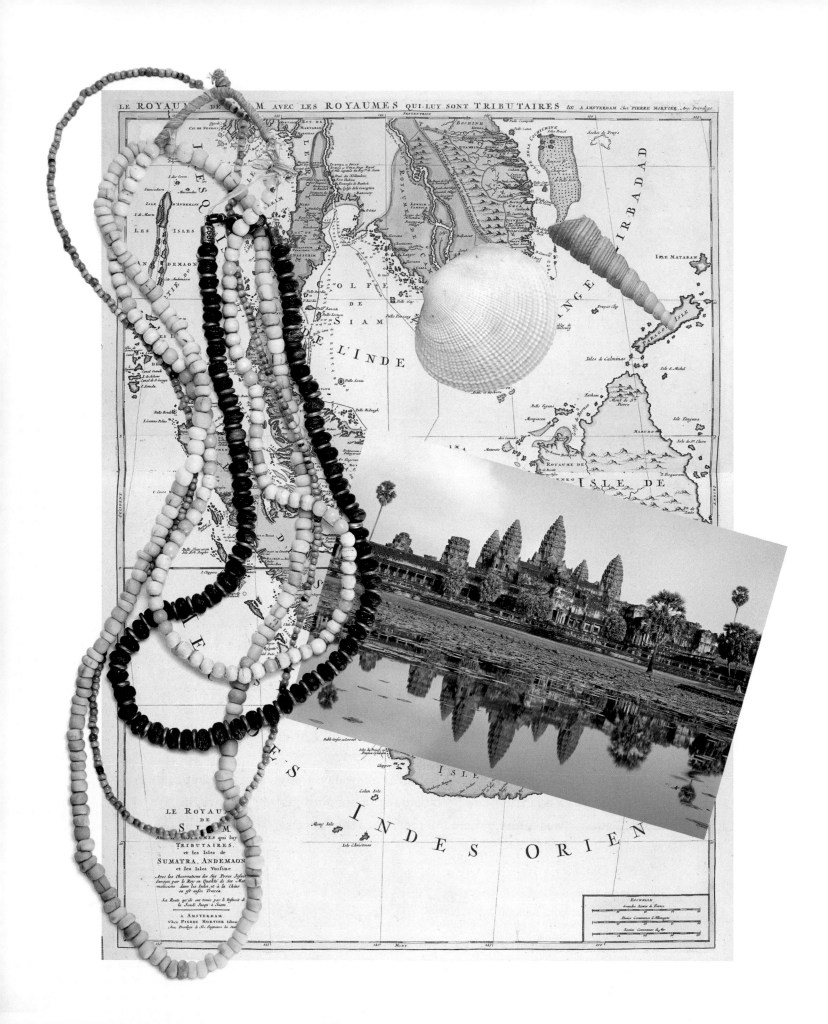

that day we talked, *really* talked, about how we had both come to this place in our lives, where we knew we were finally exactly where we were meant to be, with exactly the person we were meant to be with. Fernando was born in Argentina, the youngest of three brothers. He hadn't had an easy time with his father, and later on he'd been in a number of complicated relationships. Parts of his past clearly made him uncomfortable. On the ferry back to our hotel, he seemed to shut down, becoming distant and quiet. "What's wrong?" I asked. He was worried that he'd revealed too much to me. He was normally so confident that it was odd to see him embarrassed. The sun was out, and the sky looked like a pearl, and we sat there on the boat for a few minutes, just feeling it rock and skim across the river. "Look," I said, taking him in my arms, "wherever you have been, whatever you have done in your life, it doesn't matter. We're together now."

Our trip was full of wonder and fun and—though I didn't sense it at the time—peculiar little moments of risk. That year—2004—was the first Cambodia opened up to tourists, and when we visited the temples of Angkor, you had to make certain you stayed on the path for fear of old, buried land mines. In Siam Reap, we checked into a beautiful old hotel and set off exploring the antiques markets. At one of the temples, I remember, there was a snake in a cage with a fence around it. Two tourists were there, staring silently at the snake, and Fernando snuck up behind the man—a perfect stranger—and grabbed his ankle. The man's girlfriend doubled over with laughter, and eventually the man did, too. It takes nerve, and a huge sense of humor, to approach a stranger that way—Fernando had both.

In Colombo, our charmingly shabby hotel failed to charm Fernando, and the city was congested and smoggy, to boot. Fernando was unhappy. "I shouldn't have brought you here," he said. I told him I was fine just being with him, and pretty soon his mood lifted enough that he decided we should leave the city a little earlier than planned and drive to the beach. The water was why we had traveled all this way, right? As we drove, we passed by two different orphanages, the children playing outside in the sun. Christmas was only a few days away, and I felt that I should stop the car and try to do *something* for them, but I just didn't have the courage. I guess I was afraid of being perceived as the American who shows up unannounced and invades their space. I am still haunted by my mistake.

The Stardust Beach Hotel was owned by a Danish couple, Per and Merete, who had lived and worked in this tiny community for years. For breakfast every day, Per would bring bread fresh from the oven. It was a point of pride for him to serve

what he had cooked, and he'd stand watch over you to make sure you ate every last crumb.

Fernando and I spent the first few days swimming, sunning, reading, and going for walks, or lounging around our simple thatched hut. Unplugged? Let me put it this way: I'd never felt so far from my life in Chicago, ever, and in the best possible way, too. It took me a couple of days to adjust to the pace of beach life, but I was grateful for the opportunity. Fernando wanted this vacation so badly for us both, and I gave myself over to it. At first, I was afraid that turning off my cell phone and letting go of my email would leave me feeling lost. On the contrary, I felt liberated. I felt relieved. At one point, I remember seeing a father and his young son on the beach. The little boy was one of the most beautiful children I had ever seen. "Look at his face!" I said to Fernando. It was a magical thing to watch, this beautiful little kid splashing around in the waves, laughing with his dad.

On the third or fourth day, Fernando started going slightly stir-crazy. The place wasn't nearly as sublime as he remembered. "But I'm so happy just being here with you!" I said. "I have never done anything like this before." Still, I told Fernando that if he was really that eager to leave, why didn't we fly to South America and surprise his nieces and nephews? Fernando said he'd think about it. "So what did you decide?" I asked him an hour or so later. He told me that flying to South America would take two days, and that if I was really, truly happy there—which I kept assuring him I was—then "I guess this is where we're supposed to be."

Once the decision was made to stay, Fernando and I tried to figure out what we could do to help the children we kept seeing. In the end, he was the one who came up with a plan: We could find the twenty poorest families in the area and assemble backpacks for their children. All we needed were the ages and genders of the kids, and we could stuff the backpacks with fabric (for new clothes) and toys and school supplies. We were able to get a list of names, then we went into town for supplies, and for the rest of the day, in the shade of the hotel restaurant, we sat filling up backpacks and securing them with twine. Naturally, he and I argued over the best way to distribute them. I thought the kids should come to the hotel, but Fernando pointed out the kids had grown up nearby and probably never felt welcome at the hotel. In the end, we decided that the next day, December 26, we would invite the families to a place on the beach in front of the hotel and hand out the presents.

Our hut was simple. There was an iron bed with a thin mattress, a desk with a lamp, a chair, and hooks for our clothing. Mud brick walls three-and-a-half-feet high rose up to meet the thatch that covered the roof and the sides of the hut; a little window looked out the back of it.

Both of us were excited about the celebration we had planned for the next morning. It felt good to give something back to a place that was so lovely and hospitable. We fell asleep.

We were still in bed at around 9:00 the next morning when we heard a cracking sound. "What is that?" I asked. As if in response, water started trickling, and then pouring, into the area between the brick and the thatched roof, as if someone were emptying a giant pitcher of water over us. Fernando got out of bed immediately, and grabbed his camera, to make sure it didn't get wet. The children's backpacks we had arranged so neatly on the floor of the hut began swirling around, and the next thing I knew, it was pitch black and I was pinned underneath the bed from the pressure of the water. A few seconds later the roof of our hut was torn off, and Fernando and I were swept out of the hut by strong currents.

When something like this happens, your brain goes to a very primal place. It wants one thing: to survive. You don't ask yourself, *Where am I?* or *Where is Fernando?* You don't think, *What happened to my wallet?* or *I'm not wearing anything.* What you think about is breathing. I remember telling myself, *The only thing I have to concentrate on is the moment I come up for air. I have to take a really deep breath, and then I have to hold on to that breath.*

All of a sudden there was light again and I knew it was coming from the sky, which meant I was near the surface, so I shot up and took a deep breath before the water slammed me back under again, sometimes for twenty seconds, sometimes thirty, sometimes for maybe a minute or so, at random intervals. It happened at least half a dozen times. Gulp for air, then back underwater. It felt like being

trapped inside a washing machine. I knew that my only job was to preserve my energy so I could rise up, because *up* meant air. I knew that for reasons I couldn't comprehend water was everywhere. I thought, *I am going to die.*

Under the water, I remember forcing myself to calm down. And for a moment the currents seemed to have calmed slightly, too. I saw sunlight, and I swam to the surface. By now, I was able to swim, and also to catch my breath. Things were moving past me: babies and barbed wire, cows and cars and men and women and I was trying not to get hit or cut or pulled back under—then suddenly Fernando popped up out of the water, only four feet away from me. I had no idea where we were. I didn't know how far the water had taken us or how close or how far away we were to land. All I could make out was a sea of debris. Then things began coming into focus. I spotted a half-submerged telephone pole. I saw the jut of a rooftop.

By now we were traveling at about 40 miles an hour. The best analogy I can think of is that it was like white-water rafting over rapids, the difference being that these rapids were filled with people and enormous hunks of sharp metal and glass. I had no idea how much time had gone by—five minutes, fifteen minutes, half an hour? I saw that the water was taking us toward that telephone pole and I remember thinking, *We're moving so fast, and that pole is coming up so quickly, and if we hit that thing, we could both be knocked out.* Just then, a thin mattress from one of the hotel huts floated by and wrapped itself around that pole, so we collided not with the pole but with the mattress. "Hang on, hang on," Fernando called out. I reached over and grabbed hold of his hand around the pole. We hung on to each other, trying to resist the pull of the water. *Should we try to climb the pole?* I wondered. Then I remembered being taught as a child never to touch wires in water, and realized that if we made it to the top we'd probably be electrocuted. So Fernando and I stayed where we were, clutching each other's hands. I still had no idea what had happened, but the extent of the devastation was becoming clear. People were standing on rooftops, screaming hysterically.

"What *was* that?" I asked Fernando. "What just happened?"

He didn't know, either. "Be strong," he said to me. He said it a second time, and then a third. "Just be strong. Whatever it was," he told me, "it's all over now." A few seconds later, a second wave changed the direction of the water and slammed us both violently off the pole, propelling us backward. Fernando reached for me. I remember him grabbing for the waistband of my underwear, and missing, and then grabbing for my leg, and again missing. I was thrashing wildly, trying to swim, trying to avoid being smashed under the water.

That was the last time I ever saw Fernando, or felt Fernando. I say *felt* because he and I were always touching in one way or another. Even when we were having dinner at a restaurant, he'd adjust his body so we could be closer to each other. But at that moment I started drowning again, and the primal instinct kicked in, and all I wanted was to breathe. This time I knew there was no way I could survive whatever this thing was . . . but again I saw the sky, and again my lungs clutched for air. I broke through the surface and immediately looked around for Fernando. There was no sign of him. But I convinced myself he was going to be fine. He was a strong swimmer; he was a surfer. He'd grown up in the Brazilian jungle. If anybody could handle himself, it was Fernando.

Again, the water changed direction, and now it was carrying me back over the village. It was then that I spotted a house with a chimney. I remember thinking that if the chimney was still standing, it must be halfway sturdy. I maneuvered myself toward the rear of the house, where I treaded water for a few seconds. I was over what must have been the yard, a palm fence five feet below a rooftop. Somehow I climbed to the top of the fence, where I reached for the lowest roof tiles, boiling-hot from the sun. I knew the only way to save myself was if I could jump from the fence onto that house, climb the roof across the burning tiles, and hold on to the chimney.

The first tiles I clawed at came off in my hands, scalding my fingers. To this day, I don't know how I managed, but I did. I pulled myself up onto the roof, with my legs on fire from the blistering heat of the tiles—and I kept screaming Fernando's name. I knew with absolute certainty that any second he would reappear. I expected to hear him shout back, "Over here, I'm over here," but he didn't. Fifteen feet away, a naked, bleeding stranger sitting on another broken house was sobbing, and at that moment I realized I had blood all over me, too. Another man, floating behind the house, yelled for me to help him. I reached for his hand, but, to my horror, I didn't have the strength. He fell back under the water and I never saw him again.

TO THIS DAY I DON'T KNOW HOW I MANAGED, BUT I DID.

By now I had a 360-degree view. The water was packed with broken bodies. The sobs and shrieks were almost deafening. A Swedish woman I recognized from the village was up in a tree, and she yelled at me to leave my perch, that another wave was coming. She gestured to an area two hundred feet away, where people were struggling out of the water onto a strip of dry road. I couldn't fathom leaving the security of my rooftop and lowering myself back into the water, but then it dawned on me that Fernando must be over there, where those people were, frantically looking for me. Of course, it made perfect sense that he had gotten himself to a patch of dry land and was trying to find me. I lowered myself down and swam and waded and willed myself across to solid ground.

I kept asking people if anyone had seen a man who looked sort of like me, but no one had.

Everyone who survived had made their way to the highest point in the village, a hilltop, where a metal bridge was half suspended in the air. I made my way, too, all the while looking for Fernando. A stranger handed me a pair of shorts, and I put them on. Every place I turned, children were standing alone, crying. I stopped to ask one boy—he was 8 or 9—if he knew where his parents were, and he told me, still crying, that he didn't. "Tell me what they look like," I said, adding that the boy should take a seat in the shade, that he couldn't just wander around the streets by himself. Earlier, I'd met a British couple, both injured and both hysterical, and I knew they were looking for their child. I found them, told them I'd seen a little boy who was searching for his parents, and that he was safe, and that I knew where he was, and that they should stay where they were. Then I got the boy and brought him to his parents. This gave me hope that I would find Fernando, that any second now he would come trudging up the road.

Later that afternoon, I was reunited with Merete, Per's wife from the hotel. Per was dead, she told me. She helped find blankets. We spent that night in a field, having broken into a house that belonged to the local governor, grabbing whatever food and blankets there were, and coping with the alarming rumor that yet another wave was heading to shore. We camped in that field until the first helicopters began showing up with food, followed by more helicopters, which would eventually take us to the military hospital twenty miles away. All the while, I continued searching for Fernando, convincing myself that he had ended up on the other side of a collapsed bridge. I considered swimming across the bay, then realized I was better off staying where I was, and that Fernando would be likelier to find me if all the survivors were in one place.

When dawn came, I hadn't given up hope. But that second day was much harder. Rescuers had begun dragging bodies out of the water in wheelbarrows and stacking them in a schoolhouse across from the field. I had never seen a dead body before, and all I could do was hope and pray one of them was not Fernando. I also managed to call my mother from a cell phone plugged into a car battery, as well as a producer from *Oprah*. I told her I was surrounded by people who were wounded and children who had lost their parents, and was there anything she could do to help us or publicize what was going on? She immediately mobilized a team of producers to help me and everyone else they could. Like all the people around me, I hadn't eaten for hours—which wasn't a problem for me, as I had no appetite. I must have gone back and forth to the makeshift morgue about forty times, where I lifted up sheets to expose the faces of the men and women who hadn't survived; Fernando wasn't one of them. The rescuers were now piling up the bodies outside, since the schoolhouse had run out of room and was beginning to smell.

That day and the next, rescuers loaded the most injured survivors onto helicopters. At one point, I saw a man I recognized weeping by the side of the road. I realized he was the father of that beautiful little boy Fernando and I had seen playing in the waves. His son was dead. I stood there frozen, watching him weep. It was the first moment I said to myself, *That's going to be me.*

When it was time to board the helicopter, I resisted. I didn't want to leave without him. But the people around me advised that it would be easier to send out a search party if I were someplace with heat, electricity, working telephones, and Internet service. The next thing I knew, I was in a helicopter that had no doors, gripping a strap as we flew to the military hospital in Ampara, twenty-five minutes away. Next was an eighteen-hour truck ride to the capital, along with a slow-

One of many notes Fernando would send me by mail

moving line of cars. In Colombo, I stayed for the next week and a half near the American embassy, watching BBC news. A special security team was dispatched by helicopter from Singapore on a mission to scour the area for Fernando. There were a few false sightings. Some people had seen me, and told officials that I was Fernando. I had a working cell phone by now. Every time it would ring, my stomach would turn over, since I didn't know if it meant good news or bad. The only thing I did know was that I wasn't going to leave the country unless I could find Fernando. Instead, I made up various scenarios: Fernando was lost. He had amnesia. He was injured and he couldn't talk and he'd wandered into a nearby village and he had no way to reach me.

But every night, I lay there thinking, *This was one more day away from the day of the tsunami, and he still hasn't shown up. Where is he? Where is he? Where is he?*

Fernando used to tell everyone that he would never live past the age of 40, and everyone, myself included, hated when he said it.

Fernando Bengoechea was 39 years old. His body was never found. He simply disappeared.

I think that's exactly the way he would have wanted it, especially in light of all that I witnessed in the schoolhouse morgue. His brother Marcelo once said to me that the only thing that could ever have taken Fernando off this planet was one of the largest natural disasters in history—it took a tsunami to take Fernando from us. And so I returned to Chicago alone, back to the home he had changed for the better, the place where our lives had joined, where we'd spent so much of our time.

Since December 26, 2004, I have never defined myself by anything other than my ability to survive. I don't think about whether I'm successful, or I'm not successful, famous or not famous, busy or bored. To me, the ultimate question, the only question, is, *Can I survive or can't I?* That's what matters. I remember once talking to a friend who never seemed able to appreciate the beauty of a moment. She and I had gone to a fantastic destination wedding, and the next day all she kept saying was how she couldn't believe it was over, and that now she'd have to return to her everyday life. I had to remind her that the point of the trip wasn't that it was over, but that it had *happened*. Which is how I think about the year I had with Fernando.

Coming back to Chicago was one of the hardest things I've ever had to do because it meant acknowledging that Fernando was really, truly gone. I mean, if I were still in Southeast Asia glued to the BBC as the newscasters continued to calculate the death toll, if I were still sleeping on a stranger's floor alongside

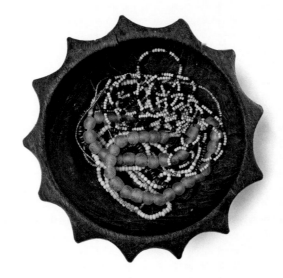

others who the tsunami had left lost and alone, if I were still fending off friends and family who were begging me to come home, well, that meant I was still *inside* the experience. Leaving meant the experience was over, that it was the past, that it had become a devastating chapter in my life, and I was now left to face the question of what the future would be like without Fernando.

When I walked back into my apartment for the first time, my mom and dad—who, as I said, had been divorced since I was 2 years old—were sitting on the sofa. They had been together for days, waiting for me to board a plane from Southeast Asia and come home. It was my mother, actually, who told me there was a high risk of airborne illnesses in Sri Lanka and that I should return to the States as soon as I could get a flight. For my health. For my safety. For my sanity.

I spent the first two weeks at home in bed, not showering, not doing much of anything, really, but sleeping when I could and crying constantly and smoking cigarettes nonstop. A doctor came by to check on me, and a psychotherapist showed up at the house every day. I had no appetite, and was weighing in at 150 pounds. Because I was on such a crazy pharmacological cocktail—the doctors at the Sri Lankan hospital prescribed antibiotics, but neglected to explain that they'd also given me Klonopin, a strong tranquilizer—it's no wonder I couldn't sustain much of a conversation with anybody.

One of my greatest comforts at that time was being inside a home that was overflowing with memories. Fernando's imprint and essence and vision—the fact that he'd flipped a vase upside down and set it on the fireplace mantel—held me together when I was coming undone. In the days before we'd left for our trip,

"I'VE ALWAYS BELIEVED THAT WHEN THE SOUL GETS WHAT IT CAME TO GET, IT GOES."

we'd had an argument about what I wanted for Christmas. By now, you've noticed that we were both pretty good at arguing and, like any two people in the process of blending their lives, we did our fair share of it. I told Fernando that the best present I could ever receive would be one of his woven photographs. Fernando had always been inspired by woven crafts. He began cutting up his photos, then weaving the strips back together so that they almost resembled pictorial textiles. He took his work from being beautiful to being something that gave back a little bit more every time you looked at it. He sliced apart a moment, and then remade it on his own terms—more intricate, more fragile, more resonant, and far more unique. At the time I made my request, all twelve of his woven photographs were on exhibit at the Ralph Pucci gallery in Manhattan. Fernando was angry and hurt that I had asked him for one. The truth was, he didn't want to sell any of them, and if he could afford to keep them all, he would have. He wanted to know how I could be so insensitive as to ask him for something he never wanted to part with in the first place? And yet the day before our flight to Asia, Fernando arranged to have not one, but two of them sent to the apartment. And when I got home that first awful night, they were leaning against the wall in the foyer.

I couldn't love those two pieces more. They represent the sacrifice Fernando had made to be with me. He and I shuttled back and forth between New York and Chicago. He always carried the strips of his photos with him in a cardboard tube and worked on them in his spare time. He'd been wanting to give up commercial photography for fine art photography, and those amazing woven photographs symbolized that goal, and his decision to share them with me symbolized the hope he had for our future.

I was deluged with condolences, some a little awkward, some a little misguided, all genuinely well meaning. But one that stands out, that I remember very clearly, was that at some point during those excruciating first weeks, Oprah came to my house. She crawled into bed beside me and listened while I cried. I kept asking, *"Why?"* It was not a rhetorical question. I needed something to start making sense.

She was quiet for a long time, then finally spoke: "I've always believed that when the soul gets what it came to get, it goes."

In that moment, I felt I understood what Fernando had come to get: *home*. Even though he'd had incredible relationships before we met, his whole life he'd wanted nothing more than a feeling of home, of security. It's what we both wanted and it's what we were fated to give each other.

When you met Fernando, you knew you were among one of the strongest, most purposeful and persistent people you'd ever meet—that he was here to accomplish what he set out to accomplish, and that if you didn't understand that, he had no time for you. He genuinely didn't get what it was like not to have his own way. He set the bar extremely high for people but never any higher than it was set for himself. Because of Fernando, I hold the people I love a little bit longer; I try to listen when I'm too tired to listen; I can't imagine ever worrying, let alone arguing, about taking three weeks off. And not a day goes by when I don't think about him. I know when he would be proud of me, and when he would be disappointed in me. And I also know that the memories I have of making a home and feeling at home with another human being—that is all part of Fernando's legacy.

Did the loss of Fernando make it impossible for me to stay in Chicago? The answer is both yes and no. Stronger than my grief is my instinct for nesting, for creating a space that feels like home. For about a year, I left things in my apartment exactly as they were when Fernando was alive. Then one day I was sitting in my living room, and I found myself wondering, *What if those chairs faced the opposite direction?* And, *What if I moved that metal bookshelf over to that wall—wouldn't that work better in this room?* Then I thought, *But I can't move them, because this is the way Fernando and I had this room.* If I moved things, I would be moving *him,* and the memories we shared in that space.

In the very next instant, I realized that moving things around and reshuffling interiors and surfaces had been a profound part of our relationship—and that the concept of leaving my apartment as it was, frozen in time like an exhibit, would have made Fernando laugh his ass off, that the best way to honor him was to follow my instincts, to mix it up and continue the experiment, just as I'd done my whole life. My home in Chicago was never about creating a shrine or a permanent collection. Fernando was alive in all the things I surrounded myself with—he still is—and for me to suspend that evolution was in fact the polar opposite of who he was and everything he believed in and everything we'd done together.

Mr Desco
5472 Mar
Hol

BRIAN SAWYER

GABRIEL

I COULD TELL YOU BRIAN SAWYER WAS BORN and raised in Indiana, that he comes from farming stock, and that as a boy he collected stones, quartzes, minerals, and whatever seashells he could find, even though there weren't any beaches for miles around. I could explain how at Wabash College he studied music and biology, before one of his professors recommended he follow his bliss and pursue landscape architecture. And that would pretty much bring us right up to the present, where as principal of Sawyer-Berson, his New York City architectural firm, Brian designs residences ranging from East Hampton mansions to Manhattan roof gardens to sprawling mountain homes in Telluride. But in telling you these things, all I'd be giving you is his bio. To really understand the life of Brian, you've got to see his stuff.

A glimpse inside his jewel-box of a foyer, which also serves as his dining room and office, tells you almost everything you need to know about this brilliant man. The classic painted paneling matches the darkest vein from his Carrera marble fireplace and offsets the black table where Brian spends most of his time blueprinting the ways for his clients to live. An ancient-looking brass chandelier that began its life in a private club or a fraternity (he can't remember which) hovers above the desk like some kind of mythological creature coming in for a landing. Against one wall is a black upright piano whose lid he hasn't opened in two years, not because he doesn't love it, but because he knows that the piano demands daily practice, and he has no time right now.

But just as you think you've got Brian pegged as a buttoned-up workaholic, you look around the room and it begins to dawn on you that he's a lot more off-center and complex than that. The objects that collude and collide in my friend's Greenwich Village apartment encompass everything from Buddhist amulets to ostrich feathers to beautiful bowls to photography to the most amazing menagerie of birds I've ever seen outside the Museum of Natural History. The truth is, when you enter Brian Sawyer's apartment, you almost want to get the back of your hand stamped.

A lot of the pleasure I get from owning something comes from telling the story of where and how I got it, what sort of deal I struck, and, of course, what I went through to get it back home in one piece. But Brian's stuff always has an aura of mystery about it. Over our decade-long friendship, he and I have ducked in and out of who knows how many antiques marts and flea markets from Milan to Mexico. The thing is, I cannot remember ever seeing Brian buy anything! I'm the guy you glare at as he attempts to stuff the Moroccan side table under his airplane seat. But Brian is exactly the opposite. He looks, he touches, he occasionally circles back and looks again, but somehow he always manages to leave empty-handed. Then a week later I drop by his place, only to find it filled with the most amazing antique brackets and ceramic figurines and coral branches and African stools and always, always, a bird I could swear I've never seen before. And that's Brian: highly strategic in all he does but (unless the two of you are riding your bicycles up to the Cloisters on a Saturday afternoon) one of those guys who never seems to sweat.

The other thing about Brian is that he's fantastically improvisational. As he explains it, "I like to find stuff and then put it in more worshipful settings." Which means that in his guest bedroom, a small Asian painting he found at a Chinese flea market in Manhattan (and which he happily dismisses as "a piece of junk") has been done up in a new black frame, with a generous silk mat, and is well on its way to dominating an entire wall. My eyes are riveted to that painting, in a way they wouldn't be if he hadn't scooped it out of the chorus and given it a starring role.

It's a reminder that sometimes presentation makes all the difference. On either side of the bed are red lacquer lamps with small clocks built into them that Brian discovered in an antiques store in Los Angeles. And at the foot of the bed there's an elegant eighteenth-century English wardrobe that Brian lined with marbleized paper. It doesn't hold much twenty-first-century-sized clothing but it makes an excellent perch for the stuffed white dove that sits on top of it, encased in glass.

Just down the hallway, Brian's "summer bedroom," as he calls it—"I admit, it sounds completely ridiculous,"—is both chic and comfortable. Mixed in with the books on his shelves are simple, circular shapes known as "bis." It is now time for Bis 101: Bis (pronounced *bees*) are small stone offerings that people tuck behind the altars at Buddhist temples. While common across the world, the most precious ones are made from either pure white or a flawlessly transparent green jade. The smaller ones are about the size of drink coasters, while the larger ones resemble old record albums. Brian owns dozens and dozens of them. "Mine are all kind of average," he says. "I go to Chinese flea markets and just start haggling."

He also collects beautiful bowls, not to store paper clips or thumbtacks in—in fact, some cost so much he wouldn't dare—but to admire as a form of everyday sculpture, especially the ones created by a friend, ceramicist Peter Lane, which combine inky blueberry colors, deep plums, and violets against a celadon glaze. He also collects and displays bowls and dishes made out of Chinese horn. "What I love most is the expression of material—rock or quartz—in this beautiful, unusual, almost translucent way."

One of Brian's most prized bookshelf possessions is an eighteenth-century courier's box that he bought at the estate sale of Evangeline Bruce, renowned fashionista and wife of David Bruce, the U.S. envoy to France, Germany, Britain, China, and NATO. It's designed to hold letters and documents, and even though Brian hasn't figured out what to put inside it, he likes the way it looks. So do I. Another beautiful object with next to no function is a thick calligraphy brush connected to a piece of red-dyed coral. It sits on the shelf beside a travertine obelisk and makes him smile every time he sees it.

In the foyer/dining room, Brian's stuff really takes flight. . . . Stuffed canaries and hummingbirds sit patiently on the high shelf that caps the molding, while an enormous goose ringed by thistles shares space with a glaring snowy owl. The birds were a legacy of Brian's great-uncle, a butcher who had a thriving side business as a professional taxidermist. When he died at the age of 102, he left Brian his entire collection. Over the years, Brian has added to what he owns, and friends have also chipped in with pheasants and songbirds. If they weren't so exquisite, the room might look like Tippi Hedren was about to stop by—very Hitchcock. But they're extraordinary, and maybe even a little melancholy.

Amid the birds, you can also find two small paintings—one by his maternal grandmother, the other by his paternal one (both of them liked to draw). Two other objects remind him of his childhood: a pair of old-fashioned dark green casserole dishes. Brian's mother used to cook his favorite childhood meal in those pots, a 1970s-era hodgepodge known as "Texas Hash," a kind of chili made with rice, cheese, and green bell pepper. As a guy who's pretty much obsessed with a little something called "Bavarian Wiener Casserole," I'm only sorry that there was no canned cream of mushroom soup involved. "Texas Hash was delicious, but it's maybe better left as a memory," Brian says, "because someone tried to make it for me a few years ago, and it was just awful. But my mother loved those pots, and I convinced her to give me three of them." He is presently using one pot to collect raindrops from a leak in the hallway, one of the bona fides of New York City life.

Behind the door is a high chair you would have sworn Brian ate from as a baby, and he would have, he insists, if he'd been born in an English country manor somewhere around 1783. Instead, he recaned and refinished the chair because he wanted to restore it to its former glory, just as he frames his collection of birds in a way that accents both their oddness and their beauty.

On the treasure-filled mantel above the fireplace, on either side of a blue-hued portrait of sky and clouds painted by an artist friend, are two glass bulldogs, one black and one white, resting on gold vintage wall brackets. Brian found the dogs at John Derian, an antiques store in the East Village that specializes in eighteenth- and nineteenth-century ephemera. They are joined by a small painting that was a birthday gift from the artist Ross Bleckner, and a second pair of moody little pugs, who gaze into the distance as if they're waiting for their master to come home. "I thought those dogs went pretty well with the Chinese theme around here," Brian says. Two more stuffed parakeets and an extremely colorful stuffed wood duck also populate the mantelpiece, along with a stern, beautiful portrait of a young Greek man created by my late partner, Fernando Bengoechea. "It's one of my very favorite things," Brian says. Mine, too.

Another treasure Brian brought home from the Evangeline Bruce estate sale is a tiny ink drawing of the Hotel de Crillon in Paris. It rests on three old brown-leather books. Two tall brass church candlesticks flank the fireplace, and two more large circular bis rest against the marble. The effect is incredibly calming.

Brian designed the classic black desk in his foyer. "I wanted the same leather as my cordovan shoes. It's my favorite table. And it's my absolute favorite place to sit." On one edge of the desk rests something called a "scholar's rock"—a naturally occurring piece of coral-like stone formed by the movement of water and tides. Scholar's rocks come in all sizes and colors, and weigh anywhere from twenty to two hundred pounds. "They're objects of contemplation," Brian explains.

The roots of that passion—the first rocks, shells, and minerals Brian began collecting as a boy—sit on a tray in the foyer. Next to it is one of his favorite things, a pale white plaster bas-relief of Oscar Wilde in profile. Brian and his mother

found it in an Indiana antiques store, and when it hit him who it was, he realized
. . . well, you can't *not* buy a profile of Oscar Wilde in the middle of Indiana. And as
long as you're exhibiting stuff that you just plain like, you might as well put out
a tiny pristine white skull, and a small bowl holding what looks like dust, but is
actually the crushed stone remains he brought back from an active Guatemalan
volcano. (The soles of his shoes melted, but he got his rocks!)

In Brian's ceiling is a large skylight made out of blue, green, and pale yellow
glass. When the sun is overhead on long summer days, the colors refract the light
and send it shimmering around the room. Two oversized black-framed mirrors
whose glass has been deliberately aged hang on the walls, one of them reflecting a
sculpture of two intertwined lovers that, I want to be charitable, sort of reminds
me of the famous scene on the beach in *From Here to Eternity*—if Burt Lancaster
and Deborah Kerr had been played by two large lumpy brown chestnuts. "Everyone
hates it but me." Brian shrugs, adding defensively, "I thought it was interesting."

Actually if it's interesting you want, then nothing beats the two packets of sky-
blue letters with lacy handwriting on them, delicately knotted in black string.
They look like envelopes sent home from boarding school, or camp, but they're
not. In fact, Brian isn't even quite sure whose letters they are. He discovered them
at a junk shop, and brought them home for safekeeping. "When I bought them, I
thought to myself, 'I wonder what's inside there.' But I've never dared to look.
I figured it was invasive enough to own them, so I told myself I would never read
them. I would protect them." Just beyond the letters, two very striking green vases
elevated on stone plinths can be found on the fire escape. "I keep them there as a

reminder of the garden I don't have," Brian tells me. "Every year the co-op board threatens to call the fire department and make me remove them." For now, at least, they continue to bring a touch of country life to Manhattan.

Brian's diaries are on the top shelf of his bookcase, accessible only by a stepladder. (If there was ever a fire, he assures me, he would snub the owl, the canaries, and the hummingbirds, grab his diaries, and run like hell.) He hides other volumes elsewhere in his apartment, and now and again he'll dive into one of them. "It's twenty years of my life," he says simply. "And I like seeing the musical notes, annotations, and ideas I've inscribed during the years I spent studying music." Next to those diaries is a vintage black Chinese painter's box that holds an Indonesian puppet, the sort that jerks around on wooden sticks. "I keep the box locked," Brian says. "I was afraid the puppet might come to life." I have to admit, I'm sort of relieved.

Are any of us as uncomplicated as we think we are? Do our design styles ever follow a straight line? I don't think so. We inherit the DNA of what we love and though we can reject it or accept it, it will always form the earliest foundation of who we later turn out to be. What's most fascinating to me about Brian's space is how a childhood love of rocks, minerals, and sky has evolved into the completely

grown-up landscape of light and stones that inhabit his interior. How a great-uncle he barely knew created the birds that look down from shelves and cabinets, alongside a couple of vintage green casserole pots that, granted, may never again see the likes of Texas Hash, but still remind him of the best parts of a Midwestern childhood. And how a batch of unread letters will remain, forever, a batch of unread letters.

I can now throw out a guess as to why Brian's space is so mysterious. It's because this very outgoing yet private man reveres the enigma of who we are and who we become. On his watch, a simple piece of stone on a tray is allowed to surge, a sand-dollar-shaped Buddhist amulet makes your jaw drop, and a bird that once raced through the night becomes a lovingly detailed miracle. The stones soar, the birds can't, and yet they both come to life. Brian Sawyer may design spaces for a living, but he is also an architect and a curator of all the people he has ever been, and all the things he has ever seen, loved, and held on to.

"WHAT I LOVE MOST IS THE EXPRESSION OF MATERIAL."

BARRI LEINER GRANT

WHEN I FIRST WALKED INTO BARRI Leiner Grant's new apartment off Chicago's Lake Shore Drive and saw the chipping vintage bookshelves in her foyer, I almost didn't need to see the rest of the place.

"This is you right here," I told her. And honestly, I couldn't love anything more. The shelves spill over with mirrors, vases and figurines, framed family photos, vintage wooden boxes, Eiffel Towers in various sizes, and stacks of fashion and design books. There's a collection of heart-shaped rocks, a little jade necklace, a pair of loving cups, a funny-looking owl, even a steel horse bit that you would swear was made by Gucci. And, of course, to know Barri is to know that there's always going to be a plate of shells she brought home from the beach.

A writer, photo stylist, jewelry designer, and mom, Barri could care less about the big stuff. The thing she is passionate about is what I call the "smalls"—a tattered ticket stub from a great evening out, a party favor from a night she couldn't stand to see end, a handful of yellowing dice in a quartz holder guarded by a thumb-sized Scottie. The bookshelves in her foyer are the perfect landing pads for Barri's mementos and an opportunity for her to tell the story of who she is.

She's a hunter-gatherer, one of those diehard souls who wakes up at dawn on a sub-zero Chicago morning, grabs a hot cup of coffee, woolly mittens, and haunts the outdoor flea markets. The dealers all know her by name. They look for her, wait for her, even set aside a shell-encrusted dish, or a rusted capital letter "B" for her.

Since just about everything she loves comes from a flea market or a yard sale, the home she was looking for in Chicago had to have enough character to support her things. A modern glass box just wouldn't do it. She eventually found what she was looking for—a vintage light-filled apartment with original moldings and old metal doorknobs that serves as the life-sized jewelry box for the trinkets and memories she lives with every day.

What I love most about Barri's apartment (aside from the fact that almost nothing in it is new) is that the rooms are both handsome and playful. The walls are painted pale gray to offset the apartment's glossy white moldings—a color combination that always looks expensive—but she's turned everything on its ear by throwing in an ottoman reupholstered in shocking pink. That's very Barri. Even after fourteen years of friendship, she can still throw me a shocking pink curveball that I just don't see coming. Her space always makes me think of a very elegant banker wearing a chalk-striped suit with funny socks. It's filled with individual moments that knock me out. An old branch sitting on top of a bookshelf? (I can't remember who did that first, Barri or me, but it's in both of our homes.)

Barri's two favorite words are *magical* and *memories*. These words come up a lot when she talks about her late mother. Ellen Jane Leiner was fun and glamorous, a petite, head-turning babe, stylish in her Jackie O. dark glasses. "My mom polka-dotted our lives with places, experiences, with her words, and with love," Barri says. Whether it was squeezing in an extra hour on the beach as the sun went down, or splurging on lobster at a local diner with her two girls by her side, or waiting impatiently every summer for her favorite Santa Rosa plums to show up in the local supermarket, Ellen Leiner always made room for a good time.

"For my mother, the gas tank was always veering toward empty," says Barri. "She was just constantly soaking life up. She used to say to my sister and me, 'Lean forward, girls, we're running on luck.' . . . She had a giant personality, and she led a big life. And today I say that exact same thing to my own girls."

The Jersey Shore, where Barri grew up, in the late '60s and early '70s was miles of old-school boardwalk linking one town to the next. It was pebbly jetties extending out into the waves, where boys and men fished and hauled in crabs. It was a not-so-ritzy beach club with cabanas where a teenage girl could slather on the Coppertone and change into her bikini. It was beachfront snack bars selling burgers and hot dogs, and lots of arcade games. And when summer was over, and the population thinned out, long afternoons spent on the beach gave way to chunky wool sweaters, pumpkin patches, and farms glimpsed from the backseat of a station wagon. It was a place where a kid could have fun for free.

Barri and her mother spoke every single day. So when her mom died of cancer at age 50, Barri, then 26, was devastated. She remembers attempting to sort through and preserve the essence of her mother, but it was tricky. "You could fit in the palm of your hand what my mother physically left behind," Barri says. "A few trinkets and bits of jewelry here and there. She wasn't a saver, not a keeper of things."

Which is why, more than almost any other home I know, Barri's interior is the one most linked to her past, and to the memories she wants to keep alive, not just for herself, but for her two daughters—Emma and Quinn. "I took a 360-degree turn from my mother's design style, in that old, dinged-up things mean a lot to me. My mother was more 'Live it, don't chronicle it.' The difference with us is that Emma and Quinn keep a record of what we do together as a family—whether it's a receipt, a seashell, or a playbill from a show we saw." And all these souvenirs are *displayed*.

A magical mother and the spirit of a childhood "spent on vacation" are alive in every room. The apartment isn't just a place that injects the spirit of sunshine-yellow flip-flops into a residential Midwestern neighborhood. It's a home that evokes the breezy memories of a childhood spent on the beach. The apartment may be some 700 miles away from the nearest lobster trap, but it looks like a weathered house atop a sand dune, a place that's been in the same family forever. If it had a driveway, that driveway would be made of broken oyster shells. Barri's apartment is filled with memories and things that her own two daughters can literally have, hold, and pass on to their grandchildren and great-grandchildren. I think of my friend as a first-generation legacy-maker.

One of the things I love most about Barri is her stylistic freedom—her ability to transform every single space in her house into a tableau that showcases the things that matter most to her. For example, one wall of her office has been transformed into a visual Grand Central Station, a wall thumbtacked with vintage postcards, I ♥ NY bumper stickers, place cards from dinner parties, quotes you instantly want to commit to memory, faded watercolors painted by her daughters, and sweet notes from old friends. Barri didn't scour the aisles of a superstore for the perfect mass-produced magnetic strips or bulletin board, either. She just unrolled a wall-sized piece of cork and painted it white.

Outside that back office, the rest of her space is all about silvery shells, gray rocks, and low tide. The beach and her love of vintage things show up in every piece she chooses for her home, from a simple scallop shell in a silver dish to a sheared beaver pillow she had made from her mother's old fur coat. "I can smell her perfume when I think of her in that coat."

We often look to other people for permission to do things in our homes that haven't occurred to us. I love taking something a person will never use anymore—the only one who needs a mink coat in 2012 is a mink—and turning it into a luxurious pillow that brings back the memory of a beautiful mother you'll always miss. Why not tie a piece of twine around an antique glass decanter, or perch a branch atop a bookshelf, just because you happen to like the way these things make you feel? Why not fill your home with old rocks and shells and pieces of driftwood you've scooped up from the shore?

Barri's shells are everywhere—on side tables, mantelpieces, and windowsills; in cookie jars, silver bowls, and chipped porcelain dishes. Every little set of shells represents an actual trip she and her family took together. The mist-colored scallop shells on the side table beside the couch are from Nantucket. A bowl of darker shells were found on the beach in Ocracoke, on the Outer Banks of North Carolina. One time, Barri—who is incapable of giving anyone a thoughtless gift—brought me twenty seashells, stacked from the tiniest to the biggest. They were wrapped in a little cellophane bag tied with a red-and-white gingham ribbon, and came with a vintage postcard on which she explained that she and the girls collected them on the beach for me. Those shells reside in my bathroom to this day. Another time, she gave me a small silver matchbook, engraved with a "B," for *Berkus.* "You don't know how hard it is for me to part with this," said B for Barri. Believe me, I knew, which is why I love it all the more.

Probably my favorite moment in Barri's home—the moment that makes me covet her personal style—is the chalkboard she's placed above the fireplace mantel in the living room. How many mirrors and paintings and flat-screen TVs have we seen above fireplace mantels? Putting an old black chalkboard in a plain wood frame above the mantel, and then having your kids draw on it whenever they want, feels spontaneous and imaginative and liberating. It's a confident move, and when you think about it, you can't really have personal style without confidence. You have to decide who you are and what you like.

On one wall of the living room is a display of silhouettes of Barri's daughters in wood frames (one with a water stain across it, which, no surprise, Barri loves). Taken from actual sittings, they're romantic, stylish, and whimsical all at the same time. On the floor below the cluster of silhouettes sits an antique dollhouse, which Quinn filled with tiny, antique sticks of furniture, along with a couple of babies that look an awful lot like space aliens. The dollhouse may be missing part of its roof, but it looks like someone's grandfather made it. "I never grew up with a dollhouse—I think my mother would have freaked—but I always liked dollhouses at other people's places, so I found dollhouses at flea markets for my daughters."

In the dining room, beneath a vintage crystal chandelier, is a massive wooden table that I gave Barri as a present, surrounded by custom-embroidered 1960s Baker chairs that came from an old Grand Dame apartment on Lake Shore Drive. At one point, the embroidery was a dramatic orange, but time, and years of sun off the lake, has faded its blaze. What can I say? We both like them better this way.

I see a lot of people struggling to make their spaces slightly unreal, to keep the actual life they lead *out* of their homes. I'm not a big fan of that, and neither is Barri. She thrives on imperfection, she celebrates all major flaws, she brings in real life in a way that's unexpected and honest, and kind of great-looking.

Above a tricycle parked in the dining room hang three weathered, wood-framed vintage maps of Maine, Chicago, and New Castle, Delaware, which Barri found in various flea markets over the years, with each representing a place she has either lived or vacationed in her life, while more shells lounge in a nearby antique tray. Inside an old bead-board cabinet in the dining room is one of her most prized possessions—a monogrammed glass Tiffany pitcher that her father kept in his office when Barri was growing up.

"I never asked him for it, but I always loved that pitcher from afar. On my dad's last visit, he gave it to me. It was like magic—and today I fill it with flowers." Barri, who calls herself a "monogram maniac," likes the rounded, engraved 1960s *Mad Men*–era type that makes up her father's initials.

In a nook of the kitchen hang some of her daughters' framed stick-figure paintings and drawings, including one that says, "Momie, I love you because I like you," and a 4-year-old girl's feminist anthem: "I am a wimin."

When they first moved into the apartment, Barri told her two daughters that they could paint their bedrooms whatever color they wanted, with one stipulation: The color had to come from the beach. Emma went with a surf-blue for her walls, while Quinn decided on a lighter Nantucket-blue. Mixed in with the "Peace" and "Love" signs dotting both bedrooms are leopard-print sheets; antique quilts; sock monkeys; bead-board cabinets and hutches; a flea market "restaurant," with its own fridge, stove, and sink; more shells; water glasses brimming with fresh tulips; and even a fat vintage Tiffany whale silhouetted against a windowpane.

"Ever since my girls were little, they've each kept what I call 'memory boxes,'" Barri explains. Opening the lid, she starts sorting through things. "These are progress reports from school. Here's a candle from an old birthday cake. Here's a ticket to some concert or other." Recently, Quinn brought home a ticket from a ball game, all crinkled in her back pocket, so she could save it in her memory box. "She's starting to make her own memories. And you know something else? Both girls will probably collect shells for the rest of their lives."

Even if your story lacks storybook continuity, as most of ours do, a place, a home, and in some cases, a feeling—can be as unbounded as an Atlantic beach. We cherish the best parts of the past in different ways. If Barri's mother polka-dotted her childhood with places, experiences, words, and love, Barri is doing the same for her own two daughters. Summertime can be transformed into a bowlful of scallop shells. A late-day breeze can become the creased wall map of a much-loved vacation spot. The memory of a mother's appetite for life lives on in a family who will continue collecting memories together. In the end, "everything finds its place," Barri says. "That's what home really is to me."

"OLD, DINGED-UP THINGS
MEAN A LOT TO ME."

KELLY FRAMEL

I T ALL BEGINS WITH A GAZELLE WHO
goes by the name of Fiona. This extremely regal, but very
demure, brass figure with pointy antlers lounges on a smoked-
glass coffee table in Kelly Framel's intimate Williamsburg,
Brooklyn, living room, eclipsing all that surrounds it, including a
black-and-gold deco table lamp, a small metal sculpture that looks
like it recently fell to earth, a fat white candle, and a stack of oversized
design books. Fiona takes in everything: the two overlapping black-
and-white cowhides on the floor, the simple white sofa decked out
with gold metallic–trimmed throw pillows, the black-shaded floor
lamp whose long neck arcs over a nearby armchair, the Lucite dining
table that can seat six without taking up any space visually, and a
black-and-white leather ottoman that looks like it came straight from
the Casbah.

As the guy with a stuffed leather rhino head mounted on the wall of his bathroom, I'm not about to question the presence of a golden gazelle in another person's space. And though I may have swiped that rhino head from my mother's basement in Minnesota, while Kelly and Fiona hooked up on eBay, neither Kelly nor I would ever consider making a move without them. "No matter what changes around here, Fiona always has a place of prominence in my life," Kelly tells me as she shifts her brass friend's position an inch or two to the left. "She brings a lot of glamorous energy to the space."

In fact, Fiona epitomizes the very glamorous, very female, very vintage energy of Kelly's apartment, but she's also willing to share the spotlight. Flea market treasures, design photos, offbeat artwork, mementos from Kelly's Austin, Texas, upbringing—yep, that's a hog's jawbone on the small Lucite table, a gift from Kelly's father, who found it on a hunting expedition—and, of course, the jewelry. When she's not focused on Glamorai, her fashion blog, Kelly collects it, designs it, and revels in it. I believe it was Confucius who said, "If you choose a job you love, you will never have to work a day in your life." That line seems custom-made for a woman whose life is her work, whose work is her life, and whose very chic interior is a combination of the two.

Kelly is one of the very few people I've seen who has actually managed to turn a run-of-the-mill (think tasteful, yet generic) newly constructed apartment into a home layered with color, texture, and enough quirky little surprises to make it completely her own. It's not easy to take a shell and create something vibrant, let alone—and this is a word I don't just throw around—soulful. But by focusing on blacks, whites, and golds, she has created a sensuous, candlelit interior that mixes a little bit of *Boogie Nights*, a little bit of "Bohemian Rhapsody," and a whole lot of personal style.

If the hog's jawbone from Dad didn't make it clear, I can tell you that Kelly comes by her love of stuff naturally. As a girl growing up in Austin, she—and her parents and her extended family—liked two things: going to open houses and scouring flea markets. Whether through luck or premeditation, the Framel ancestral gathering place happened to be close to a gargantuan flea market, and when they weren't eating turkey or stuffing stockings, the family spent practically every end-of-year holiday browsing and haggling, so it's no wonder that the woman was born to bargain. When she isn't haunting vintage stores in Brooklyn and Manhattan, or slowing down in front of yard sales in the Hamptons, or digging

for treasures online, she's prowling flea markets across New England to ensure that Fiona will always have plenty of company.

Take the trio of paintings hanging in her living room. The first shows two children huddled together —"That picture reminds me of my old roommate and me," she says—the second is a preliminary sketch of what will eventually become a drop-dead chic party dress by a designer from Banana Republic, where Kelly has been a consultant, and the third is a portrait of Kelly that an antiques dealer made one day when she was poking around his showroom. It seems to me that the picture looks more like a really grizzled country star than a really stunning Kelly Framel, but it's the thought that counts.

Then there's the portrait of the striking, milky-skinned girl gazing dolefully into space. Who is she? Well, whenever Kelly and her friends make their thrice-yearly pilgrimages to a Massachusetts flea market, they spend the night at a nearby inn whose interior is filled with turn-of-the-century paintings of children. But not just any children. In the early twentieth century, Kelly explains, traveling artists/salesmen pre-painted children's bodies, then went door to door in search of parents who wanted a portrait of their kids. Wasting no time, the artists would paint the real heads onto their canvases. "It's an extremely weird sub-genre of early American art," Kelly says. "My friends and I like to call the paintings at the inn where we stay the 'ghost babies.' So when I found this at a flea market, I knew I had to have it."

Every square inch of that home is well used, and well loved. Kelly's desk is populated with candles, an incense holder, and a giant brandy snifter crowded with matches from restaurants, nightclubs, and hotels. A dazzling 1970s-era silver-and-gold sculpture hangs on the wall, giving off a kind of ironic Bee Gees vibe. Kelly found the piece at a Massachusetts flea market, and aware that C. Jeré pieces were selling for up to $10,000 online, was more than happy to pay the $140 asking price. Somewhere outside Boston, a flea market proprietor is sobbing into his clam chowder.

As for the bedroom, how gutsy is it to hang a giant longhorn above a perfectly pristine queen-sized bed? She found the three-foot-long steer horn online, and though I'm not from Texas, seeing it makes me want to lasso something and drill for oil. Even more fantastic are the two mannequins beside the bed, dripping with beads, necklaces, belts, and medallions, some of them Kelly's own designs, others just stuff she loves wearing. On one wall are two framed black-and-white pictures

Kelly tore out of *French Vogue*. They complement the old chest of drawers she got from Craigslist, sanded down, and painted into a black-and-white piece that could have fit very nicely in Christian Dior's atelier. On that chest she's laid out a sparkly tableau of vintage bowls overflowing with bracelets, necklaces, candles, an inky-black skull candleholder, and a lamp that on closer inspection reveals itself to be a woman with long legs that reach up into a lampshade skirt. A black wastepaper basket in the shape of a snare drum (another yard sale find) completes the picture.

Kelly has also transformed her utilitarian kitchen into something fresh. She found the Lucite chairs on the streets of Brooklyn and draped lush pieces of sheepskin over their seats, which took them from vaguely uncomfortable to I'm-so-happy-here-I-will-never-stand-up-again. Instead of stuffing her silverware and glasses inside a drawer or behind a cabinet, she has hung rows of clear floating shelves on one wall, anchored by a plain plastic planter. For a moment you can almost believe you're gazing at a contemporary art installation. Her forks, knives, and spoons are divided into a row of glasses on the bottom shelf; flea market glasses are lined up on the next shelf; another row of glasses sits on the middle shelf; vintage spice jars make up the next; and a collection of glossy white ceramic pieces top it all off. Kelly's cheese board is a vintage black-and-white granite chess set she brought home from a Hamptons yard sale. "I don't always like to use things the way they were intended to be used," she says, pointing to a container with a gold reindeer-head lid that she stores her tiny Pyrex measuring glasses in. I've always been a sucker for anybody who tries to think outside the gold reindeer head.

If your bathroom lacked the space for a full-length mirror, what would you do? Kelly has positioned hers on the hallway wall outside the bathroom. Then, in order to deflect attention from the fact that she has positioned one there, she

hung nearly a dozen vintage mirrors around it. In a ground-floor apartment where the shades are perpetually drawn for privacy, the mirrors give her space light and a sense of fun . . . that is, if you define *fun* as cutting up a scrap of Ralph Lauren fabric and decoupaging it over the frame of one of your mirrors, using Mod Podge glue. And if she's ever running short on shampoo, or soap, she can jot down a reminder on the slate board she keeps in the hall of mirrors, grab her favorite hat from the white bust sitting by the board—the bust looks like a Roman philosopher in training to become a drag queen, thanks to the feather and turquoise necklaces he's modeling—and take it from there.

"It matters a lot to me that I have a clear separation between my living and working spaces," Kelly says. She's managed to achieve that separation through a staircase topped with block letters reading, "Your Day Will Go the Way the Corners of Your Mouth Turn," which ushers her into a beautifully organized office.

When most of us hear *office*, we turn a little schoolmarm-y. We think, *I must have a grown-up desk. And I need a serious lamp.* And even *I will invest in a chair that twists and turns and puts people on hold while notarizing forty-six documents and making lunch reservations.* It's like we believe that installing major office furniture communicates gravity and purpose. I love Kelly's workspace so much because it encourages pure play and genuine creativity. Stones and gems and bead-filled glass jars and shallow bowls, multicolored spools of thread, and wall hooks filled with rings and garlands are all there for the taking. It makes me want to become a jewelry designer in my next life, or maybe even later in this one, but at the moment, I feel like I'm inside an amazing retail store where I just want to buy *everything* I see.

A pretty white chair covered with another sheepskin is Kelly's command central, and to circumvent the built-in concrete columns, and with an assist from IKEA, Kelly installed custom-cut white countertops along one wall. On another wall is a shelf lined with silver reindeer that sit beside yet another mannequin (this one is wearing sound-blocking gold earphones), a beautiful black-and-white shot of Kelly, and several very graceful hand mannequins pointing and gesturing as if they've been possessed by Vanna White. Another wall is devoted to books and white filing cabinets, along with a vignette that includes an Asian basket, a painting of a dog, and a worn-looking octopus with four stringy red legs. Yes, a child could have made it, but it's actually a Kelly original, created from an old skirt and a little imagination. "I call it 'Glamour Monster,'" she says.

My favorite thing in this room has to be the tall, skinny theater marquee signs Kelly found in a Broadway Dumpster, presumably after the show in question had closed. One reads " 'Devastatingly Funny!'—*The New York Times*" while another reads, "Frantically Cheerful!" She found the signs on her way to a job one morning, and arranged to store them there until she could find a pal with a truck. Forget remembering birthdays and sending chicken soup when someone has the flu, real New Yorkers understand that lugging theater marquee signs from Midtown Manhattan to Williamsburg is the mark of a true friend.

Give your space personality! I can't tell you how many times those words show up in TV shows and magazines dedicated to design. The thing is, a lot of people take that as a signal to start poring through catalogs, scouring online websites, and incorporating the latest trends. We forget that *personality* means "us." It turns out everybody's mother was right when they said those three little words, *Just be yourself.*

Which is one reason why the stuff Kelly has chosen to bring into her home is so inspiring to me. I mean, c'mon, a gazelle named Fiona? A sculpture that could've shined down on Liza as she discoed the night away at Studio 54? Candles and beads, bangles and bows, belts and medallions, a jawbone downstairs, a longhorn upstairs, and thick swatches of sheepskin almost every place you sit? By stocking beads in clear jars, hanging hooks on the wall to display her latest inspirations, and looping tangled lengths of chain wherever it feels right, ideas leap into being. Kelly's work and her surroundings are so magically aligned, I can almost guarantee she never has to work a day in her life.

KELLY AND FIONA HOOKED UP ON EBAY.

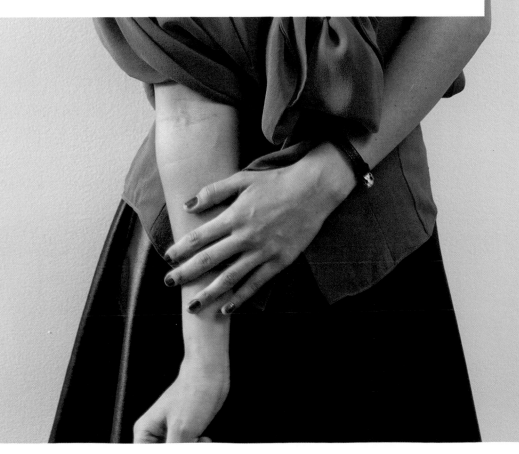

STEVE BERG

H OW MANY PEOPLE CAN YOU POINT TO in your life who really get you on a deep, spiritual level? I've been fortunate to make a few friends who have no particular agenda, who love unconditionally, who are happy to celebrate when things are going well, but manage to stick around for the dark days, too. No doubt about it: Having somebody who understands what's truly in my heart is an incredible gift—but having somebody who understands my head of hair…well, that's a miracle!

Steve Berg has been cutting my hair for the better part of a decade. On days when I was in front of the camera hosting my talk show, Steve was there, brandishing his brush and flat iron the way a gunslinger wields his Smith & Wesson. Together we've seen our share of snowed-in airports and greasy fast food joints, but every now and then we pulled into a new city with a little extra time to kill. And that's the moment Berg and I would hit every vintage store, antiques mall, and flea market within a thirty-mile radius. The secret to our shopping success? We never reach for the same thing.

Because his one-bedroom Greenwich Village apartment is so small—maybe 450 square feet—Steve has to be exceptionally careful about the stuff he buys, which is my definition of both a blessing and a curse. Mick Jagger said it best: "You can't always get what you want." But the flip side of Steve's limited space is that it has forced him to become a ruthless editor, which means he has created a home that holds only the things that really speak to him. And two things that speak volumes to Steve Berg are surf and sand.

Steve may be a New Yorker through and through, but what he values above all else is nature, and it shows in nearly everything he owns. His stuff is rustic, textured, and earthy, and it would look every bit as good in a Montauk beach shack (which is where I suspect he'll eventually end up) as it currently looks in his Manhattan co-op.

Take the skeletal dolphin tail hanging in his living room. "I found that in a thrift shop on the Outer Banks of North Carolina," Steve tells me. "Then I started to worry: *Are they killing dolphins for their bones now?* I asked the woman behind the counter. She looked at me like I was some kind of tuna-boycotting city slicker and explained that nobody was out there hunting for Flipper. It turns out her husband found it one morning when he was walking their dogs along the beach. And that was that. My theory is, if something actually washes up onshore, then it was meant to be."

The piece hanging directly beneath the dolphin tail is a beautiful bleached-out wood frame that Steve filled with a mirror. "The bones of this apartment don't have a lot of character; they're not particularly homey, so I had to find ways to create some warmth," he says, pointing to the old frame holding the new square of glass. The mirror is anchored by a mid-century modern walnut dresser. It's one of those classic Danish pieces on hairpin legs that looks a lot more expensive than the $400 Steve paid for it at a giant warehouse in

SCAVULLO ON BEAUTY

SCAVULLO ON BEAUTY Francesco Scavullo

BARELLA

Stratford, Connecticut, that's filled with booth after booth of great stuff. "Every time I check that place out, I feel like I'm taking a tour of somebody else's life. It's like visiting a great museum."

Steve has instinctively learned a design lesson that a lot of people seem to struggle with: When an item can be old, go ahead and let it be old, but if you can't get your hands on the right vintage piece, then it's perfectly fine to buy something new. His sofa, in a quiet oyster-colored linen, is new, but it's got a wonderful worn-in quality and a timeless style that makes it seem like it's been part of his life forever. It's also a really good size. "I frequently feel like my sofa is just too big but I've got to have comfortable seating when friends come over—it even functions as a twin bed when someone needs a place to crash for the night. I've gotten a lot of people through a lot of bad breakups on that thing. Besides," he adds, "one day it dawned on me that having a small space doesn't mean all of my furniture has to be small." His cable-knit sweater pillow is something I designed a while ago, and Steve had two black ikat-print pillows made from fabric I brought back from Thailand as a Christmas present for him. My thought was that this fabric would fit right into Steve's space because, like everything else at Château Berg, it's understated yet intricate, classic yet cool, restrained, charming, and always slightly unexpected.

As you can see, Steve has a very refined sense of what he wants in his home. I admire that. Like me, he's drawn to worn wood and tarnished metal and natural fibers. Some people have a fear of flying, some fear heights, and even Superman was pretty uncomfortable around Kryptonite. I'm guessing the thing that would totally freak Steve out—his Kryptonite—is patent leather. He just can't deal with anything too shiny or plastic-y. The Danish bench, with its original black woven leather top (nothing patent about that leather) works as either a great little coffee table or a place to put your feet up and read the paper. He uses the teak bar cart next to the sofa as an end table. It took a while to find one that he both loved and could afford, but he managed with a little help from eBay.

I love the juxtaposition of his vintage brass stool next to the woven rush chair. The white rubber dining chairs are Italian, from the early 1970s. Steve paid $140 for the set of four at the same place in Connecticut he got the Danish dresser. Notice the way he's paired them with his glass-and-chrome dining table—they balance each other perfectly. I also love that Steve doesn't use his dining table strictly for dining. When space is limited, it helps to have stuff that serves more than one purpose. He's got books, shells, starfish, a wooden vase with a rich grain, and a vintage desk lamp

on his table. He's also got a couple of wood rings that look as if they came straight from the 1950s. The truth is, they came straight from West Elm.

Above the dining table is a photo that Steve came across on a shoot with me at Parsons School of Design. "The students are tremendously talented but their work is still very affordable. This is a shot of some old junkyard and I guess I was drawn to it because it's such a nice combo platter—very urban, but there's a lot of nature there, too."

The black kilim rug with cream and gray stripes pulls the entire room together. He found it on a website and bought it on the spot. I'll be the first to admit that I'm a serious enabler—I can always make a case for something beautiful—but as far as this rug was concerned, he really didn't need a push from me. Steve has always been careful with his money, but when something is absolutely right, he doesn't hesitate. I learned that the hard way one day when I made a rookie mistake and momentarily forgot what I've been preaching for years: Antiquing is not a team sport!

You know how early in the chapter I said Steve and I never reach for the same stuff? That's what any shrink worth his prescription pad would call "denial." That amazing triangular mirror above the sofa? Steve says he falls in love with it over and over again—which is exactly what a good piece of art should make you do. The mirror is ceramic, although it reminds Steve of whale bone; it might have been done in the 1930s or, for that matter, maybe the '50s or '60s. It could be that some wildly talented person took an art class in Aspen and had it hanging in an upstairs bathroom. Or it's possible that an artist created the piece and it sat in a Chelsea gallery filled with showier stuff that eclipsed its subtle beauty. There's something very romantic about imagining the origins of this mirror, but the truth is, I don't have a clue who made it or where it came from. All I know is that Berg got to it

before I could, which, let me tell you, made for one very long and extremely quiet car ride home. . . .

As for the other pieces grouped above the sofa, trying to curate that collection was Steve's biggest design challenge. "Do you hang the stuff you most identify with, or is it all about the scale of the different pieces?" he would ask me. I urged him to just experiment, but he kept saying, "I've only got three walls in the living room, so there's really nowhere to mount a TV, or position bookshelves. I have to be really mindful of what I put up." In the end, it was me who did the putting up. When you've got my hair, you can't afford to have the guy who cuts it distracted—so I grabbed a hammer and we got the job done.

He found the black-and-yellow German poster that advertises an art exhibition sticking out of a trash can in front of the Cherry Lane Theatre on Commerce Street. The icy blue abstract of sailboats is by New York artist Mitch Ferrin. Berg has a real affinity for the sun and the water. I always relate to that. The tramp art three-dimensional eyeglasses on the wall are very idiosyncratic and they're very Berg.

That graphic landscape to the right of the tramp art is also very Berg—literally. He made it himself using white charcoal over black acrylic paint. It's both dramatic and delicate. It's also proof that while he may identify himself as a hair and makeup guy, Steve Berg has the soul of an artist. As a child growing up in

Commack, Long Island, Steve's dream was to become a fashion illustrator or a cartoonist. "As a kid I was constantly drawing on my bedroom walls. Some guys had that poster of Farrah Fawcett in the bathing suit hanging in their bedroom. . . . I had a Farrah poster on my wall, too, but it was a sketch I did myself, and I put her in a peasant dress. When it came time for my Bar Mitzvah, I knew we'd be having a lot of company over and I wanted to spruce things up a little bit, so I painted a two-tone, high-gloss stripe in chocolate brown and tan all the way around my room, just like the one I'd seen on *Welcome Back, Kotter*." I wince at the thought of it but Steve assures me things could've been much, much worse, "My parents' bed was made out of almond-colored Formica with a strip of mirror trimming the base and an 8-track tape player and speakers built right into the headboard!" As if the Farrah thing hadn't made it perfectly clear, he adds, "I'll always be a child of the '70s."

And he'll always be driven to design. In fact, every few weeks, Steve and a couple of friends get together for something they call "art night." "Instead of meeting to dissect a book we've all been reading, or play a few hands of Texas Hold 'Em," Steve explains, "we put on some music, open a good bottle of wine, and just go for it—we paint, we draw, we sculpt, we doodle, we create."

Steve is the guy who's out there finding rocks and shells to glue onto place mats for his friend's wedding on the Long Island Sound. He's the guy who grabs a Sharpie and some spray mount to dream something up for a vintage frame he's found for six bucks at the thrift shop he scours a couple of times a week. He's the guy who studies the geography of a face and knows exactly how to design a haircut that complements it, and he's the guy who understands that in order to feel creatively fulfilled he has to set a night aside every now and then to make something beautiful happen.

He's made his kitchen beautiful by keeping it very simple. The stainless-steel cabinets and appliances would've looked good twenty years ago, and they'll look good twenty years from now. I also like how he's put everything in the kitchen on one level, which makes for a very clean, utilitarian line. When you've got only a single shelf in your kitchen, you damn well better decide what kind of stuff deserves to be on that shelf. In Berg's case, it's a vintage Danish creamer with little cups and their original wood saucers. Also sitting on that shelf is a vintage photograph, a little bit moody, a little bit desolate, that Steve calls "Serial Killer/Lake House."

He's a huge fan of photography and he's got two more eBay pieces from the 1950s hanging in his bedroom. Both shots are black-and-white and both are in thrift shop frames that he paid next to nothing for. One picture shows an Airstream trailer hitched to a car on the edge of a lake. "I'd never want to own a trailer like that, but I wouldn't mind dating somebody who's got one," he says. The other photo depicts a middle-aged couple surveying the wreckage of a tornado or a hurricane or some sort of disaster that has clearly leveled their home. You can see the flood waters rising as they hold hands in stunned silence. To me, the shot is brimming with sorrow. But that's not what Steve sees when he looks at it. "There's sadness but I also think there's something a little hopeful about the scene. I always imagine them starting the next chapter of their lives together."

The photos hang over a very simple drafting table made of wooden easel legs and a narrow glass top. There's a fantastic vintage lamp on the desk, very organic-looking, with a driftwood base that's been treated with a resin technique that was popular in the 1950s. He pays his bills at that desk, while sitting in an old schoolhouse chair. On the other side of the room is a round mid-century modern wood mirror and another painting by Mitch Ferrin: In this one a blonde in a bikini looks toward the horizon as swimmers splash in the waves. "Ferrin's work has a paint-by-numbers quality that takes me back to my childhood," he says. I'd say

there's a pretty decent chance that Steve was a Santa Monica surfer dude in a previous life. He's even got an old Hawaiian skim board leaning against the wall. "It doubles as a TV tray when I treat myself to breakfast in bed," he tells me. And speaking of the bed, it's a platform upholstered in sand-colored linen and it used to belong to me. I kept it in my guest room but when I moved into my current place, I decided that I didn't need it and Steve did.

There are two areas of the apartment that we haven't talked about. The first is Steve's hair salon. It's a very compact station in the entry, consisting of a mirror with lights running down each side, a drawer that comes out of the wall underneath the mirror, and a vintage chair he found at a garage sale.

The other space serves as Steve's oasis, his lounge, his backyard, his veranda, his porch, his patio, his campsite—or, as it is known in New York City, the fire escape. "I keep a window box out there, so I can always have something leafy around. I watch the shadows and light change all day long. It's shockingly peaceful out there."

Actually, his whole place has a certain serenity to it. There's something to be said for *not* painting, for the purity of dark wood floors and white walls; Steve doesn't have to reach for a color to tell his story. And while he lives with a lot of things, his place never feels overwhelming; almost like a Joseph Cornell diorama, where nothing is extraneous. For a man who is forever searching websites and antiques shops, tag sales and flea markets, this home is as much about what he's left out as what he's included. There is no flash or noise here. What remains is vintage Berg: mirrors that reflect back like the water, a few pieces of driftwood, melancholy old photos, sun-drenched paintings, and a fantasy of someday catching the perfect wave.

HE HAS CREATED A HOME
THAT HOLDS ONLY THE THINGS
THAT REALLY SPEAK TO HIM.

CHRIS GARDNER

Nel Mandela

CHRIS GARDNER BOUGHT HIS VERY FIRST home just a few years ago, at the age of 53. For the two and a half people left in the world who haven't read his memoir, *The Pursuit of Happyness*, or seen the Will Smith movie based on it, Chris may have taken a longer journey than others to come home—but he finally got there.

Born in a rough North Milwaukee neighborhood, he eventually found his way to the West Coast, where he began working as a medical supply salesman. One day in 1980, he saw a cherry-red Ferrari pulling up in front of San Francisco General Hospital. Chris, who as I pretty quickly found out isn't shy about talking to strangers (strangers aren't shy about talking to him, either), asked the owner two questions: "What do you do for a living?" followed by "How do you do that?"

He soon became a brokerage trainee. But when his ex-wife left him with sole custody of their 18-month-old son, he found that his training stipend couldn't cover both the cost of daycare and a place to live. While he saved up money for a place, Chris and Chris Jr. spent the next year surviving on the San Francisco streets. By day, he'd make two hundred cold calls from his desk at work. At night, he and his son sought refuge in homeless shelters, public parks, under Chris's desk at work, and even inside a locked bathroom of the train station connecting San Francisco and Oakland. None of his colleagues had any idea.

Somehow they survived. And in 1987, seven years after first catching sight of that Ferrari, he founded his own brokerage firm, Gardner Rich, which today has offices in Chicago, New York, and San Francisco. He's become a symbol of power and success, ambition and accomplishment—a CEO, entrepreneur, philanthropist, inspirational speaker, and internationally bestselling author (to date, *The Pursuit of Happyness* has been translated into forty languages).

So there's the ninety-minute Hollywood version of Chris's life, but behind that is a self-made man who has seen and thought about *home* from every conceivable angle, and who decided to trust me to design the place where he would be putting down permanent roots. I took that responsibility very seriously.

I'd never designed a home for a person who'd been homeless, though I did have an idea of what it might be like to watch your world disappear right before your eyes. When I traveled to New Orleans with the *Oprah* crew after Hurricane Katrina, I met people who had lost everything. They were carrying around the few pieces that were salvageable—clothing, a photo, whatever else they managed to grab before the storm hit.

After the tsunami in Sri Lanka, I knew what it was like to have absolutely nothing, albeit briefly. I had no clothes, no toothbrush, no wallet, no wristwatch, no soap or towel or pillow, no ID, and no access to any of those things. I didn't have a dollar to my name in any currency. Somebody lent me a pair of shorts to put on after several hours of walking around stunned in my underwear. For a person who rejoices when people surround themselves with objects that have meaning, I understood for a short, terrible period of time what it felt like to have nothing— and it changed my perspective on the importance of "things."

Before he bought the apartment, Chris had been living in a dark loft in an industrial section of town, with nothing more than a mattress and a pair of speakers as tall as he was. He wasn't used to having furniture or a proper dining

room. He'd eat at the kitchen counter without giving it a second thought. "I felt like Batman," he told me with a laugh. "But as you let go of certain parts of your life—that darkness, that sense of not wanting to be social—you start to come into your own. Leaving that place and finding this one was like coming out of the dark and into the light."

After a lot of long conversations with Chris, it became clear what I *didn't* want to create: a house that was trendy or transient or in any way unfinished. This new apartment had to have richness and it had to have weight. I needed his new home to feel grounded and comfortable for him, a place where he could put his feet up and unwind. My goal was to build a road map—an object-filled landscape that would help him tell his story in the most beautiful way possible. That means we had to plan out the "why" and "what for" of each space and every single piece.

This was going to be Chris's home, filled, for the first time in his life, with stuff *he* could choose. He wasn't bringing anything with him from his old apartment. He'd given the very few things he had to the Salvation Army and Goodwill. The only thing he'd never part with was a favorite black-and-white picture of his late mother, Bettye Jean.

"Will Smith told me that if you don't protect your private life, chances are good you won't have one," Chris explained. "I'm in an airplane seat more than half the year. So coming home *matters* to me probably more than it does for most people." In the end we created a flowing, light-filled, opulent, modern, refined bachelor pad, filled with vintage leather chairs draped in African throws, souvenirs from his many travels, and photos marking the highlights of his extraordinary life. The apartment may float high over Chicago, but I wanted the objects in it to convey substance, stability, and masculinity.

Probably more than any client I've ever worked with, Chris fully embraced what we were trying to achieve. "You really got me. I mean, you really understand me," he said when we were done. It was one of the best compliments I've ever received.

The light in the apartment streams in from a ten-thousand-square-foot balcony—the largest private balcony in the United States. For Chris, that terrace sealed the deal. The balcony looks out over the whole of Chicago. And when I say Chicago, I mean skyscrapered, Mrs.-O'Leary's-cow, I-want-my-porterhouse-steak-blood-rare Chicago! Directly ahead stands the looming Jeweler's Building, with its oversized clock; the story goes that Al Capone once ran its restaurant as a speakeasy. To the left is the city skyline, with Lake Michigan beyond it. Twenty-nine stories below you can see North Michigan Avenue, the Chicago River, and the 1920s-era terra-cotta Wrigley Building. But despite all the street-level hustle, the only sound you hear at this altitude is the lake wind ruffling the grass.

Normally, when I'm working for a client, I present the design for four or five rooms at a time. But not with Chris. He needed to see a single finished room before he could proceed to the next. Part of my challenge was to keep reminding myself that change can be overwhelming and a brand-new home represents a giant change for anybody, let alone Chris. He needed to acclimate to his stuff, and I needed to make sure I wasn't rushing him. This is a guy with very strong opinions. (I always find there are two kinds of clients—the ones who ask no questions at all, and the ones who ask the *right* questions. Chris knew exactly what to ask.) He needed control over the process, which meant taking life one room at a time. Because Chris's world revolves around his work, we began with the smallest room in the house, the library.

The library had white walls, a wood floor, and the flimsy French doors typical of new construction. It was way too cookie-cutter to be Command Central for Chris Gardner. But what if we created freestanding bookshelves with bronze trim, I asked Chris. "What if we found a metal desk for you—say, iron, with a hand-tooled leather top, imported from England, a modern variation of an antique partner's desk?" I had him at "iron with a leather top."

I'd come across a tortoiseshell wall covering a while back and decided to hang on to it for just the right client—Chris was definitely the one it was meant for. Tortoise is a great pattern, just as classic as zebra and leopard (think of all the old books you've seen bound in that pattern), but a little more unusual. I used it to cover the library walls and give the room character.

Then I got rid of those standard French doors and replaced them with floor-to-ceiling metal ones. He wound up loving their heft, and the handles set into their own metal frames. And in the end, those doors convey permanence—even majesty.

In *The Pursuit of Happyness*, Chris writes about the role that quiet has played in his life. "Stillness has always been my refuge and my defense," he explains. "Even later, as an adult, I would cope by being still. Very still. It's where I go whenever there's too much chaos around me." Chris's library exudes luxury, order, and that necessary stillness.

Even here Chris questioned me about every design choice. *Why sconces on either side of the bookshelf? Why not something heavier?* I explained that we needed a more refined touch to balance out the weight of the bookshelves; otherwise, I told him, the place could end up looking like a restaurant.

Two years earlier, unbeknownst to me, Chris had asked one of his heroes, Dr. Maya Angelou, *If you could read only a hundred books your whole life, what would they be?* "She wrote me out a list—and every book on that list is on the bookshelf behind my desk. The day I got that box of books, I can't even begin to tell you how excited I was." The black bookshelves also hold vintage and first-edition volumes ranging from *The Autobiography of Malcolm X* to Thomas Wolfe's *You Can't Go Home Again.* "The funny thing is, the first three books on the list she gave me were written by *her.* 'Hey,' she told me, 'I started alphabetically!'"

In the course of the decorating process, Chris bought an eight-foot-long chocolate-brown leather sofa he wanted to place across from his TV. We had a few back-and-forths about the sofa, but Chris told me it was a nonnegotiable point—"This area is college football central," he said—I took a deep breath and worked around it. And the truth is, I eventually came to respect and, okay, even like that sofa. It's extra-deep, and we made pillows out of vintage Mexican textiles for it.

This football-watching zone is next to Chris's state-of-the-art kitchen. The kitchen walls are painted British royal navy blue, which makes you feel like you're in the hold of a great clipper ship. Chris's daughter, Jacintha, who's an interior designer, came up with the color. Chris remembers, "When Jacintha first used the name *British Royal Navy Blue*, I said to her, 'What the hell does that mean?' But I absolutely love it." The dark blue is both surprising and restrained. It absorbs and deflects the hot-and-cold extremes of a Midwestern climate, and also complements the starburst fixture overhead, the bronze rectangular table, and the sculptural 1970s floor lamp. Keeping an eye on the kitchen from a red alligator frame is a foot-high black-and-white photograph of Chris's mother, the one he took with him to this new home. A white shawl covers Bettye Jean's shoulders. Her glance is direct and knowing, and she's smiling.

"This kitchen is *her* room," Chris says, adding that he got some of the greatest lessons he's ever learned in life in his mother's Milwaukee kitchen. Her son may have traveled far from his beginnings, but even during his first years of professional success, Bettye Jean kept him grounded. When he got his investor's license, Chris remembers calling her with the good news. To hear him tell it, his mom wasn't entirely sure what an investor's license was, but even if she had known, it wouldn't have mattered. She did what mothers do: She invited him to come over for a home-cooked meal.

Bettye Jean isn't the only person who stands watch over the kitchen. I noticed that Chris is a big fan of 1940s films—particularly the movies of Gable, Cagney, and Bogart—and I suggested we mount his favorite photos (his mom, his kids; his granddaughter, Brooke; as well as ones of him with Oprah Winfrey, Will Smith, Nelson Mandela, and Sidney Poitier) all in black and white.

The dining area off the kitchen is as sleek and inviting as the kitchen itself, and dominated by a heavy octagonal table made out of petrified wood. In one corner sits an Italian 1970s-era cabinet that doubles as a bar. I love this combination, particularly the counterbalance of heavy and light. The vintage lamp, a sliced geode, was popular in the 1960s and '70s in Europe. I also like the balance of the family photos sitting on top of something so substantial, with the mirror-framed mirror hanging above it.

The clean, spare living room is pretty much ornamental—"You will never, ever see me walking on this carpet," Chris says today with a laugh—a vintage sofa, and a 1970s Italian coffee table has a bronze base that mimics the edges of the doors. Two hand-carved chairs frame the black-marble fireplace.

And then there's the entry. Chris keeps his favorite stuff in an antique hand-carved display cabinet with claw feet. Among his treasured possessions are two metal crosses. The Pope blessed one of them during a private visit to the Vatican, and the other is a primitive sculpture of Jesus on the verge of ascension. There's also a pink seashell from a part of the Ghana coast known as "The Point of No Return," where slave ships were loaded, and where the imprisoned human cargo had their last glimpse of home. "I'm not entirely sure how, but when I was visiting Africa, that little shell got stuck in my shoe," Chris told me. "I said to myself, 'This isn't an accident, you are supposed to have that with you.'"

His all-time favorite piece is an image of a black hand against a white backdrop. It's not just any hand, it is the handprint of Nelson Mandela. Inside the open palm is a shape that looks like the African continent. The piece is simple and striking, and it's called *The Hand of Africa*. Chris traveled to South Africa for the first time more than a decade ago. His local hosts had made arrangements for him to meet Nelson Mandela, and when he finally came face-to-face with the South African president, Chris recalled, Mandela smiled, put out his hand, and said, "Welcome home, son."

"I was 44 years old at the time," Chris says. "I was a guy who grew up not knowing my real father. The first man in my life to show me any kind of real welcome—to say, in fact, 'Welcome home, son'—was Nelson Mandela."

Also on display in this case is a simple glass canister filled with soil. On a later visit to South Africa, Chris paid a call on Nelson and Winnie Mandela at home in the Johannesburg township of Soweto. Winnie told him that at the height of their anti-apartheid activities, they knew the government had bugged their house, so she and Nelson used to go out to the yard to talk privately. When the government took Mandela away, Winnie didn't want to give government officials the satisfaction of hearing her cry, so she would go out to the yard to weep. "Her tears are in this soil," Chris says. "I asked the gardener, 'Can I have some of that dirt?' The gardener probably thought I'd only take a handful. I took home eight pounds."

As a man who'd ably fielded every curveball the world has thrown him, Chris was ready to make a clean break with the past and imagine a new home high above the city that he loves and that loves him back. He is on the road two hundred nights a year, so it's no wonder that he seeks the solace of a night at home, a place that combines the sophistication of the Miles Davis music he worships; the taste of a meal on the banks of Lake Maggiore; the color, vibrancy, and joy of a South African street; the stillness of a summer afternoon; and the inspiring presence of the men and women who have shepherded Chris through the downs and ups of his remarkable life story. This home, his first, also has a power and charisma that mirror its larger-than-life owner, a man who says he wouldn't swap a moment of his great big life for anything.

"COMING HOME MATTERS TO ME PROBABLY MORE THAN IT DOES FOR MOST PEOPLE."

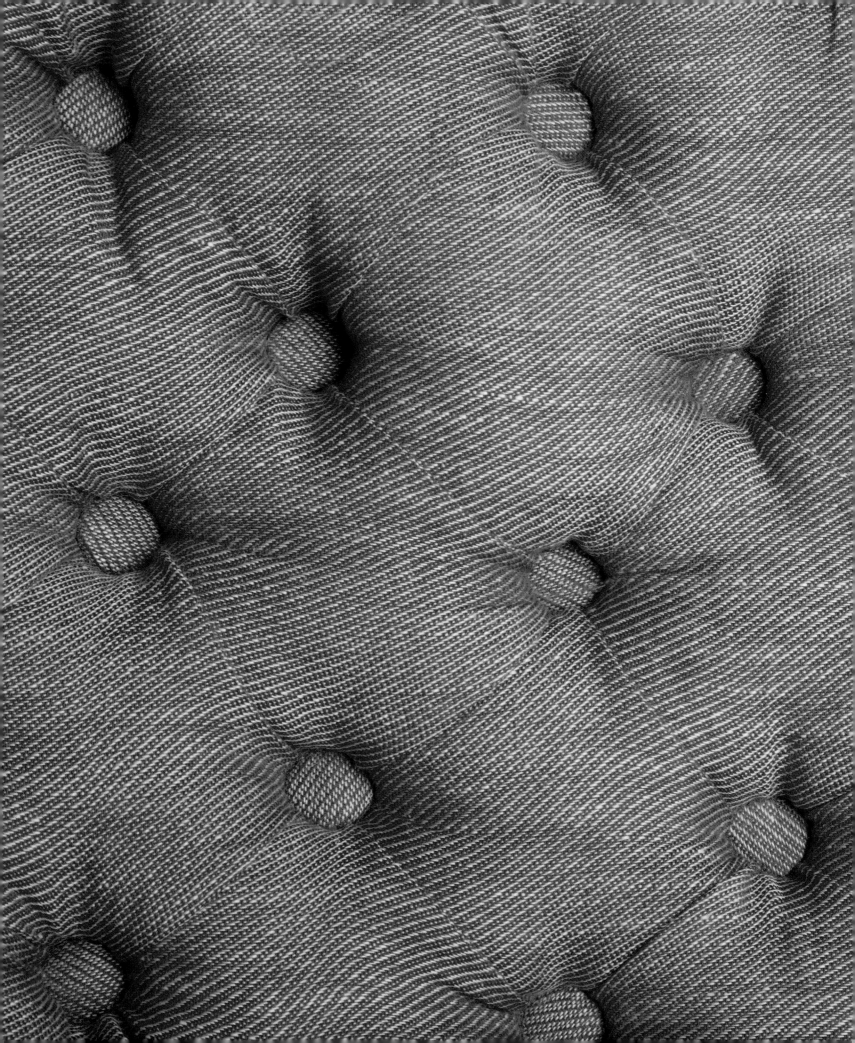

DR. RUTH WESTHEIMER

WHEN I WAS A KID, THERE WAS NO *Will & Grace* on TV, no movies about ordinary people who were gay, no books or billboards or magazine articles or anything else that simply said: You can love anybody who you want to love without fear or guilt or apology. And then along came a four-foot-seven-inch force of nature with a thick German accent and a Betty Rubble laugh who went by the name of Dr. Ruth, and suddenly for me and millions of others struggling to find their place in the world, it was a whole new ball game.

Dr. Ruth's voice on the radio was like rain in the middle of the desert. Well, actually, it was like explicit, judgment-free guidance laced with compassion, humor, and some much-needed common sense. I would lay there in my twin bed on Sunday nights, listening as sex therapist Dr. Ruth Westheimer, in her no-nonsense yet incredibly brave way, gave everyone respect, acceptance, and permission to be exactly who they were. She was a very good friend to me long before I ever met her.

When you do finally get to meet the people you have admired from afar, they don't always turn out to be who you hoped they'd be. But Dr. Ruth does not disappoint. She's funny, frank, completely down to earth, and I think it's safe to say that the woman who went on *Letterman* to extol the virtues of a good vibrator does not embarrass easily.

Yet when she told me she felt "stuck" and asked if I'd consider stopping by her apartment to give her a little free advice, she seemed a bit self-conscious. "I'll do my best to clean up before you arrive," she said, adding that if she didn't do some serious pre-visit decluttering, I'd probably have her "admitted to Bellevue." Then she hit me with a major caveat, "Oh, and you can only help me reorganize—you cannot tell me I have to get rid of anything. I just need you to say 'Put this here and put that there.'"

There are those who might consider that kind of restriction to be a deal-breaker, but I'm not one of them, and Dr. Ruth knew it. She sensed she could trust me right off the bat because I clearly love a challenge, I obviously love her, and as you're no doubt starting to realize, I've spent a long time thinking about the relationship between people and their things. This was my chance to figure out exactly how to marry living gracefully with a lifetime of collecting.

Dr. Ruth was waiting for me at the front door of the three-bedroom Upper West Side apartment that she's called home for more than half a century. She wasn't exaggerating about the need for crowd control; this is a woman who has lived a great big life, and she's got the stuff to show for it. Her place is jammed with papers (she taught at both Princeton and Yale), books, Judaica, pictures, Hummel figures, pottery and ruins excavated from who-knows-how-many archaeological digs, teddy bears, an eclectic selection of porn (she calls it "erotica," but hey, tomato/tomahto), an old-school cable box, a TV, several remotes that appear to be prehistoric, too many awards to count, and tchotchkes as far as the eye can see: the overwhelming ephemera from years of travel, reading, writing, lecturing, and, of course, teaching.

But the first thing that caught my eye was a redbrick dollhouse, much like the row houses that line Brahmsstrasse, a street in Frankfurt, Germany, where Dr. Ruth's mother, Irma Hanauer, and her father, Julius Siegel, had lived with her grandmother, Selma Siegel, when she was born. Seeing it, I assume this very impressive dollhouse is for her grandchildren. I'm wrong.

At the break of dawn on January 5, 1939, Karola Ruth Siegel, then a 10-year-old girl, was taken to a railroad station along with approximately one hundred other German Jewish kids bound for a children's home (some would call it an "orphanage") in Switzerland. She stood on the platform, determined not to break down as she said goodbye to her mother and her grandmother and everything that ever felt safe or normal, or like home. Her father was not there to see her off. Six weeks earlier, several men in shiny boots entered that small ground-floor apartment on Brahmsstrasse, and quietly insisted that he come with them. Karola stood at the window and watched as he was loaded into a truck filled with other men whose only crime was their Jewish faith and taken away. He looked back, waved, attempted a smile. She couldn't know it at that moment, but it was the last time she would ever see her father.

"The dollhouse is for me. A friend made it," she said. I took a closer look and noticed the tiny gold plaque engraved in regal cursive—"Dr. Ruth Westheimer, Sex Therapy"—hanging on its front door. The pieces of furniture inside were extraordinarily detailed reproductions, made between the two World Wars, and bought mostly in England. "You see, I grew up with no control over my life. At the Heiden home in Switzerland, the German Jewish children like me became the maids for the Swiss children. We cleaned their toilets, made their beds, scrubbed the floors, did all the laundry, helped them bathe. . . ." Dr. Ruth's voice trailed off, as she gazed at the dollhouse.

"Being an only child in my parents' house, I was always a little spoiled. I had roller skates and a wooden scooter and chocolates and a lot of love—I had thirteen different dolls." Again she paused, lost in the memory. "I was allowed to take only one doll to Switzerland, and I ended up giving it to a little girl on the train; she was even younger than me and she couldn't stop crying. Then I had none. But," she went on, as she nudged a delicate chair up to a tiny table with her thumb, "now I can play with my dollhouse whenever I like and"—she brightened—"here I have control. Everything is exactly the way I want it to be in this house."

I saw it as my job to try to bring that same sense of order to her apartment. But first I had to see the things that had meaning for her. The two of us set off on an impromptu hunt for buried treasure. Books were everywhere; they ran the gamut from *The Art of Florence* to *The Art of Seduction* with some Amos Oz and Jean Piaget (the renowned developmental psychologist was her professor when she studied at the Sorbonne) thrown in for good measure. Dr. Ruth is the author of thirty-four books herself, and as a result I am now the very enlightened owner of a signed copy of *Sex for Dummies*!

Our next stop was a miniature table resting by a pile of papers. "I have friends who used to have a gallery on Madison Avenue. And one day I saw this little table and I just fell in love with it—it's three hundred years old. My friend sold it to me at a special price but then he said, 'I want you to know that it has a crack in it.'" She traced its surface with her fingertip. "I said, 'Listen, it's three hundred years old, it can have a crack!'"

She also showed me a ridiculously tall hat made of glossy black feathers that looks almost sculptural. "Isn't it fantastic! I gave a talk to 150 Jewish cadets at West Point. I didn't take any money for the lecture. I did it to honor them. For me the Allies and the military are very important. If they hadn't entered World War II, I wouldn't be alive. The cadets gave this hat to me, I guess as a thank-you. My grandson couldn't get over it."

Wherever we turned there were photographs: Ruth with her children, with President Bill Clinton, with Mayor Michael Bloomberg, with the Duke of Edinburgh; Ruth receiving her doctorate from Columbia University; Ruth dancing with Zubin Mehta; Ruth playing tennis; Ruth paddling in a kayak; Ruth dressed as Charlie Chaplin, surrounded by a family decked out in bumblebee costumes;

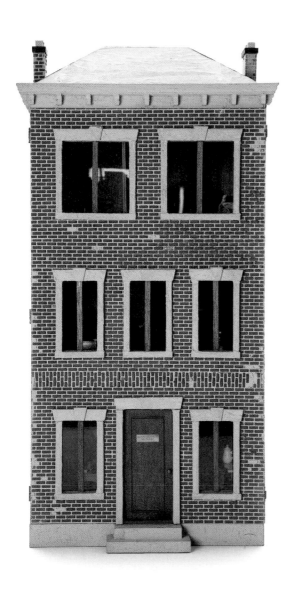

and my personal favorite, Ruth with Sir Paul McCartney. "I'd never met him," she told me, "but we were both at a Yale commencement ceremony—I think he was getting an honorary doctorate—and he recognized me. He said, 'Ruthie!' So I said, 'Sing me a song!' And he goes, 'She loves me, yeah, yeah, yeah!' I didn't have a camera but there was an Associated Press person there, and that picture went all around the world."

There were also a few more reminders from Ruth's past: a certificate documenting the fact that she has been trained as a Swiss maid ("This way when I'm not Dr. Ruth anymore, I have a fallback," she said with a laugh), and two luminous black-and-white portraits, one of Ruth's mother and the other of her father.

"So you have nothing else from your life in Frankfurt?" I asked as we looked at the old-fashioned portraits of her parents. She hesitated. "I could only take one small suitcase to the children's home. I wish I had brought more from the house, Sabbath candlesticks, a plate—anything. But I didn't because I was sure that my parents would be coming to get me, and I'd have my life back again." She went into her bedroom and returned with one small item in a plastic bag. "Because I gave my doll to that child, this is all that I managed to keep from our home."

She handed me a washcloth, a nubby blue-and-white rectangular mitt that she's cherished for nearly seventy-five years. I asked why she keeps it hidden away in a drawer in her bedroom, and she explained that she's willing to talk about being orphaned by the Holocaust, but it's not something she needs to have staring her in the face every single day. She will not be consumed by that experience.

I'm struck by a Marc Chagall piece, mystical and color-saturated. "This print is just a page from the Sotheby's catalog," she explained. "It didn't cost me a thing but surrounding it with the elaborate frame gives it an expensive feeling." I asked if she's seen the famous stained-glass windows Chagall did in the late 1950s as a gift for Jerusalem's Hadassah Medical Center. "I've seen them," she said. "But they didn't exist when I was a patient at the hospital." I had no idea she was ever a patient there. "Come sit down. I'll tell you a story."

"When the war was over and I turned 17, I left Switzerland," Dr. Ruth began. "I moved to Israel, but German Jews were thought of as people who failed to see the writing on the wall. I think the fact that they didn't get out when they should have was looked at as a weakness. Maybe that's why they were so insistent that we change our 'German' names the moment we arrived. But denial is a funny thing—I

couldn't comprehend that my parents and grandmother were really gone. I was worried that if I invented a whole new name for myself, my family wouldn't be able to find me. So I began using my middle name for my first name, and I took the 'K' of *Karola* as my middle initial. I made myself into Ruth K. Siegel. I also joined the Haganah," she said with evident pride. "I learned how to take a machine gun apart and put it back together with my eyes closed. I learned how to use a hand grenade. And I learned how to shoot; I became an excellent marksman."

This was all a little surreal for me, like finding out your grandma is part of Seal Team Six. "Anyway," Dr. Ruth continued, "on June 4, 1948, I worked my regular surveillance shift, and then at about noon I returned to the youth hostel where I was living. I remember the date very clearly because it was my 20th birthday.

"I was in the lobby when the bomb exploded. Plaster was raining down from the ceiling, sirens were blaring, people were screaming, a soldier and two girls—one of them standing right next to me—were killed. I'd been struck by shrapnel all over my body, including a piece embedded in my neck, but my feet got the worst of it. The top of one foot was completely gone and I had multiple wounds just above both ankles. The surgeons were so good at Hadassah that they didn't have to amputate."

People tend to throw the word *amazing* around all the time—I'm guilty of it myself. But if I had to sum Dr. Ruth up in a single word, that would be the one. Not only has she survived tragedy after tragedy, she has somehow managed to keep her soul intact. Where a lot of people would have shut down, Dr. Ruth chose to embrace life. It's no wonder she's my favorite pleasure activist.

As if on cue, Dr. Ruth announced, "Now I will show you the only thing in my apartment of any real monetary value." She disappeared for a minute, then returned with a magnificent diamond-encrusted gold turtle attached to a jeweled stand that in a more romantic era was used to seal letters with a wax insignia. It might be one of the most beautiful things that I've ever held in my hands. "I have turtles all over the apartment." She points to a big glass turtle on a shelf, a turtle-shaped soup tureen, a scattering of ceramic, jade, enamel, wood, and metal turtles on various ledges and windowsills and side tables. "You see, Nate," she said, "a turtle carries its house right on its back. It's perfectly safe as long as it remains tucked away in its shell. But when a turtle wants to get anywhere, it has to take a risk—it has to stick its neck out in order to move forward." She paused. "I believe in that image. It's how I've always gotten by and it's how I was able to talk about all the taboo subjects that nobody could ever seem to speak of." It's also

how she joined the underground, found love, got an education, raised a family, and became a citizen of the world. She took the piece from me, looked at it, and beamed. "This little turtle is the story of my life."

I had three reasons for wanting to make over Dr. Ruth's living room:

1. She's given me so much more than she'll ever know.
2. I wanted to show her a new way to live with her things.
3. She promised if I helped her out, I'd have great sex for the rest of my life.

If ever there was a candidate for floor-to-ceiling bookcases, Dr. Ruth was it. My solution was an entire wall of bookcases. We also found a freestanding cabinet with seven-foot glass doors—in the same classic style as the bookcases—which almost has the feel of another dollhouse. And speaking of the dollhouse, I had a stand built for it. My hope is that all these pieces will age as gracefully as the 84-year-old sex therapist . . . actually, my hope is that we'll all age that well.

When you've got as much stuff as Dr. Ruth, your eye needs a place to rest. For her walls I decided on a neutral backdrop of pale gray (to pick up her amazing view of the George Washington Bridge, the Hudson River, and the New Jersey Palisades beyond) with creamy white trim. But I also noticed that Dr. Ruth has a particular style of dressing—she's always in black slacks and a bright blouse. Because this uniform works so well for her, I decided to take my cue from it and

throw in several happy notes of emerald green, plum, coral, and shocking pink around the room. I even had her chair reupholstered in the hot pink because, like Dr. Ruth herself, it radiates joy.

I went with a simple burlap for the tablecloth and smoky gray linen for the curtains because I didn't want a pattern to fight with all those book bindings. I reframed the precious pictures of her mother and father with wide ecru mats and simple white frames so that the photos have some breathing space and the sepia tones stand out. I used gold accents in the sconces and chandeliers because Dr. Ruth is European and a hint of gold suits her. I replaced her dark, heavy furniture with some lighter pieces. I got her a flat-screen TV from this century. I also found copies of the sculptures that sat on Sigmund Freud's desk, though I suspect Dr. Ruth has a much better idea of what women really want than Dr. Freud ever did. And I couldn't help but throw in the LOVE pillow, because that's really what she's about.

Dr. Ruth has told me that she goes out five nights a week; she loves to see friends and folk dance and attend events all over the city. But I can't help thinking that she'd be much more inclined to stay home and maybe even have a few people over for dinner every now and then if her home was set up for entertaining. I designed three separate conversation areas, and made sure that the sofa is low enough to be comfortable for her. I wanted her to want to hang out.

I think we all have this misconception about our living rooms. We somehow got it into our heads that they need to be spare and formal, while the family room is the place that's relaxed and playful and filled with our stuff. But there's nothing grand about Dr. Ruth and I believe people should be able to do some living in their living rooms.

Earlier I said that Dr. Ruth K. Westheimer epitomizes the word *amazing,* but the more I went through her things and heard her story, the more I realized that word doesn't begin to do her justice. The problem was that she had so many things that meant so much to her—that reminded her of how far she's traveled—she could no longer see the forest for the trees; the things that mattered most had become a blur. I wanted to give a place of prominence to what was truly important. I wanted to take this jumble of parts and bring them back into sharp relief.

Here is a woman who'd faced brutality and cruelty and ugliness and chose to answer it with dignity and intelligence and optimism. As a child, the people and things she loved most were ripped away. I wanted her to be able to come home at the end of the day, kick her tiny shoes off, and really be surrounded by the signs of a well-lived life, the things that provided her perspective and comfort, and, for the woman whose attitude toward sex has influenced millions, nothing but pleasure.

I COULDN'T HELP BUT THROW IN THE LOVE PILLOW, BECAUSE THAT'S REALLY WHAT SHE'S ABOUT.

BARBARA HILL

MAKE TACOS NOT WAR

S HE HAD ME AT "MAKE TACOS NOT WAR." The string of six-inch-high gold letters sits above the ten-foot-long vintage cast-iron apricot-colored sink in the kitchen of Barbara Hill's home in Marfa, Texas. A perfect marriage of salvaged materials, modernism, wit, and simplicity—from the French dining room table decorated with nothing more than a plain black bowl, to the Bertoia chairs scattered around the room, to the deep bathtub sitting three feet away from her bed—Barbara Hill has style to burn. I am completely obsessed with everything about this place.

Only a confident woman with a bit of life under her belt could create a space as cool and eloquent and stripped-down as this. For years, I've told people, "Stand in your threshold and guard what you allow in."

Barbara has actually done it! She's the Stuff Police, a ruthless editor who doesn't hesitate to say, "This house isn't big enough for the two of us," as she ushers out anything that doesn't make her happy or please her exacting eye. From her kitchen counter to her closets to her bookshelves, there is no surface in her space that's not exactly the way she wants it to be. I can count on one hand the number of homes I could move into tonight, but this beautifully executed space makes me want to grab my suitcase and fill out a change-of-address form.

Barbara's home began its life as a turn-of-the-century private dance hall (yes, Virginia, along with tumbleweed and gunslingers, there really used to be dance halls in the Old West). An interior designer, former Houston art gallerist, and, before that, Miss Texas of 1956, Barbara devoted a year and a half to creating a single, open, free-flowing, high-ceilinged space. She preserved the eighteen-inch-thick white adobe walls and added overhead steel support beams. The floors are made out of birch plywood, and the fireplace and bedroom ceiling are covered with sheets of charcoal-gray industrial metal. There isn't a single drop of paint in the entire house. To preserve the spirit of life-as-it-once-was-in-Texas, she installed silver art-deco light fixtures on the outside porch. "They kind of reminded me of a theater, or a dance hall," she says.

Most of our houses have so many overstuffed containers and cupboards and drawers and storage boxes that it comes as a shock to see the naked way Barbara showcases her things. Plates and dishes are stacked and laid out on the counter and the shelves below. A creamware pitcher holds Bakelite flatware beside an old white Kodak canister filled with wooden kitchen utensils. Two closets on skateboard wheels (because, really, what woman doesn't want her closets on skateboard wheels?) keep her clothes and cowboy boots in order. Rolled-up towels fill a wicker basket beneath the bathroom sink. When our everyday stuff—plates, forks, knives, coffee cups—is arranged this matter-of-factly, we can't help but look at it in a new way. It's like "Home, Unplugged." A spoon becomes sculpture, a silvery hanger becomes a fashion statement. Barbara cares about every little thing and its effect, down to the blocky bars of white soap in her bathroom. And while I'm on the subject, can you imagine getting it so together that pretty much the only things you need in your bathroom are a couple of bars of white soap and a toothbrush? Barbara isn't traipsing down to her neighborhood superstore to buy Dixie cups and a plastic lotion dispenser, or replacing her flatware with eight gleaming new place settings.

WHEN I ASKED HER FOR THE ONE WORD SHE'D USE TO DESCRIBE HER SPACE...BARBARA ANSWERED, "POETIC."

But you can't arrive at the space Barbara is in unless you've reached a point in your life where you've pared away everything that is not essential or that you don't truly love. I know there are some people who will look at Barbara's home and maybe find it a little cold, but I would argue that the seeming austerity of her space comes straight from the heart. I call it "meaningful minimalism." The thing Barbara has figured out, that most of us—myself included—still struggle with, is restraint. She understands that we don't really need half a dozen different shampoos, conditioners, and hair gels, along with a set of towers to store them in. She has mastered the art of leaving well enough alone.

Seeing Barbara's pristine kitchen, visitors probably don't believe anyone ever eats there, but this woman likes to throw parties and, trust me, when she does she uses every single square inch of this space, even though in its off hours it still manages to resemble a stand-alone work of art. The counter features Barbara's collection of gray and brown pottery made by the industrialist sculptor Russel Wright. Tilted against the wall beside the Bakelite flatware are two plastic pancakes enclosing an extremely tiny man and woman, a piece called *Pancake Lovers* that was created by San Antonio–based artist Franco Mondini-Ruiz. Prints given to Barbara by artists she exhibited in her gallery lean against the walls, unsecured, so she can switch them around whenever the mood strikes.

One of her most prized possessions is a photo album containing pages and pages of postcards created by Japanese conceptual artist On Kawara. "I got up at 2.02 p.m.," one says. "I got up at 9.20 p.m.," reads another.

There's a story there. In the 1970s Barbara was one of only a handful of gallerists in the world to exhibit Kawara's *One Million Years*, a combination sculpture-performance in which a man and a woman take turns reading aloud consecutive dates a million years into the future and a million years into the past. One morning during the show's run, Barbara recalls, the phone rang. It was On Kawara, who was visiting Houston with his wife and wanted directions to Barbara's gallery.

JAN 30 1975

I GOT UP AT
9.52 A.M.

On Kawara
24 E. 22nd St.,
New York, N.Y.
10010

post card

BARBARA CUSACK
5120 BAYARD LANE
HOUSTON
TEXAS
77006

AIR MAIL

MAR 19 1975

I GOT UP AT
9.07 A.M.

On Kawara
24 E. 22nd St.,
New York, N.Y.
10010

Post Card

BARBARA CUSACK
5120 BAYARD LANE
HOUSTON
TEXAS
77006

AIR MAIL

"When he got back to New York a few days later, he started sending me postcards with pictures of Manhattan on them," Barbara tells me. "He sent one to me every day until— well—until he must have run out of postcards. I have sixty of them in all."

Kawara's work is spare; you notice his postcards as much for what is left unspoken as for the rhythm of his words. His pieces are all about where he's been and where he is in this particular moment, and it makes perfect sense to me that at least an album's worth of them found their way to Barbara Hill.

When I asked her for the one word she'd use to describe her space, I was prepared for just about any response. *Raw*, maybe. Or *uncluttered.* But, without hesitation, Barbara answered, "Poetic."

She's not just talking about the mood of her home; she's talking about actual poetry. A few years ago, she commissioned a friend to create a series of white coffee cups featuring some of her favorite quotes from poets and authors, ranging from Emily Dickinson to Lorca to Pushkin. "Good Morning, Midnight," says one cup, while another wonders, "Have You Heard the Whistle Long and Sharp of the Train, the Station, and the Farewells Left Behind?"

"That one is by Jean Cocteau," says Barbara. "Here in Marfa, we hear the train every night at 4:00 a.m. All of us who live here love the sound of a train rolling through. It's such a part of the Old West."

Then there are the two matching chairs in her living room. Originally covered with brown cowhide, they were reupholstered in a heavyweight white cotton. Barbara, who likes to write offbeat poetry in her spare time, spent the next week composing a pair of pulp-romantic stories that a local T-shirt company then silkscreened onto the chair fabric. It's not the first time someone in the design world has used writing on a chair, whether it's a single word or faded copy off a burlap sack of grain. But the typewriter-like font Barbara picked out makes these particular chairs sing a song that's both romantic and wry. One tells the tale of an imaginary cowboy pulling into a Texas town "on a dust storm," with "the pounding rhythm of the ride vibrating in his well-worn jeans" and "hell in his holster." The second imaginary visitor comes from back East. "She was going to take him for an art tour, but she took him for a lot more," Barbara recites. One word is even misspelled, but that's just fine—renegade passion doesn't have to dot its i's or cross its t's in her home. Hanging off two black hooks in her bathroom are two small cowboy hats, one black, the other white, symbolizing two phantom visitors. "Those hats just make me happy," she says.

HE FLEW IN FROM SOMEWHERE ON THE EAST COAST - A BLACK LEATHER CLAD ART COLLECTOR - COOL AND CRISP AS A DRY MARTINI - SHE WAS WAITING TO TAKE HIM ON AN ART TOUR BUT SHE TOOK HIM FOR A LOT MORE - HIS RESERVED DEMEANOR MADE HER WANT TO LOSE HERS....HE MOVED CLOSER AS SHE PRESSED HER BACK INTO A JUDD BOX - THE HEAT OF THE METAL MATCHING HER OWN - THE SCENT OF HIS LANVIN JACKET AND HERMES COLOGNE MADE HER DIZZY - SHE WANTED TO KNOW MORE ABOUT HIM - HIS INSIDER TRADING SECRETS....WHAT MAKES HIS PATEK PHILIPPE TICK....SHE LOST HER THOUGHTS ON MINIMALISM - AND COULD ONLY THINK OF GETTING HIM OUT OF HIS PRADA LOAFERS - HE SUGGESTE VIEWING THE MARFA LIGHTS WITH A BOTTLE OF CHAMPAGNE - WHAT WAS HE WHISPERING IN HER EAR? SOMETHING BY CARL ANDRE? AS THE LIGHTS DANCED IN THE SKY THEY FELL TO THE DESERT FLOOR IN A NOCTURNAL TANGO....

HE RODE IN ON A DUST STORM - FROM SOMEWHERE ON THE RIO GRANDE - SPURS JINGLING - HELL IN HIS HOLSTER - THE SMELL OF LEATHER AND A HORSE RIDDEN TOO FAST - HIS EMBRACE ERASING ALL TRACE OF HER ANGER - THERE WAS URGENCY IN HIS TEQUILA FLAVORED KISSES - THE POUNDING RHYTHM OF THE RIDE STILL VIBRATING IN HIS WELL WORN JEANS - THE SMELL OF A BURNING CAMPFIRE IN HIS HAIR AND CLOTHES INGNITED A FIRE IN HER SOUL - THE HAUNTING HOWLS OF COYOTES ECHOED THEIR CRIES OF DESPERATION AS THEY ABANDONED ALL TO OUTLAW LOVE - THEIR DANCE OF RENEGADE PASSION

The steel beam in the ceiling means overhead lighting is not an option, which is why Barbara installed an enormous floor lamp whose long curved neck hangs over the low, gray, extra-long sofa like an industrial grapevine. Visitors can hike their boots up on a French mail-sorting table she had cut down to coffee table level, or hang out in one of several vintage chairs sitting on the gravel-textured living room rug.

Barbara's white oval bathtub sits at the foot of her bed like a parked car. When I asked her why she loved the shape so much, she told me it reminded her of the old tubs cowboys used back when people would bathe in the middle of a room. "I can just picture a Clint Eastwood type of guy sitting in there with his boots hanging over the side," Barbara says. The bottom of the tub is so shiny it looks wet, but it's simply reflecting the charcoal ceiling above it. And if Barbara ever wants privacy from the pack of wild turkeys hanging out on her porch, she can turn the big weathered gray sign reading "Crews Hotel" into a door by sliding it across the space between the two walls.

The bed is pure Barbara—just a slab of raw Texas pecan. Once again, she has whittled away anything even remotely extraneous. I mean, what more do you really need for a bed other than a piece of wood, a great mattress, a soft pillow, and a set of clean white sheets?

On a side table Barbara salvaged from a falling-down office building in Houston sits a silvery 1960s lamp and three grainy rocks she brought back from a Marfa farmers' market. On another table is a homemade sculpture Barbara herself created using a small white car and a chunky rock. "Let me position it right so you can get the full effect," she says, placing the rock over the front fender. "There!"

Anybody who has ever driven a car through the American West will immediately understand the meaning of the crushed car. "If you drive through the Rockies, you'll see signs that say, 'Danger—Falling Rocks,' Barbara says with a laugh. "But really, what's a driver supposed to do? Back up? You can't back up. I thought it was hysterical."

My favorite little touch is the tiny pair of scuffed cowboy boots on the mail-sorting table. Barbara wore them when she was three years old. "I did some trekking in those boots, and probably some dancing," she says, "based on the look of the heels." My mother had my baby shoes bronzed, and I've been trying to scratch off the metal ever since, so it's all I can do not to jam these in my coat pocket and make a run for the border.

"The tub in the middle of the room isn't for everyone," Barbara says, explaining why she added a bathroom and separate shower to the original house. Above a vintage Irish stool—"Was it used for sheep-shearing, or shoeing horses, or tanning leather? I have no idea, which is why I like it"—hangs a movie still of a young Rock Hudson, a gorgeous Elizabeth Taylor, and a huge black stallion rearing up on its hind legs (the James Dean classic *Giant* was shot in Marfa). On the other wall is a vintage photograph of Barbara, along with forty-nine other smiling women wearing one-piece white bathing suits, shot during the Miss America pageant of 1956. She may not have won, but I like to think she was voted most likely to turn a crumbling dance hall into an amazing place to live.

I called this book *The Things That Matter* because if it is about nothing else, it's about how the prints on our wall and the rough-hewn rocks we swiped from the Marfa farmers' market give our everyday lives shape, texture, and a sense of who we are, who we've been, and where we may be heading. But the appeal of editing down our stuff to what we really need and love, and nothing more than that, is another fantasy I find myself indulging in now and then. Being able to pick up and go at a moment's notice without wondering, *But what will I do with all my things?* is a notion I find genuinely liberating. In the end, we all come into this world without stuff, and we depart without stuff, too. In the meantime, because we're human, we fill our shelves and our lives with objects

A CONVERGENCE OF BIRDS
Original Fiction and Poetry Inspired by the Work of Joseph Cornell
Edited by JONATHAN SAFRAN FOER
D.A.P.
JOHN CAGE
SILENCE
WESLEYAN / 628
BUTTERFLIES
3 WARNE
FRESHWATER FISHES
FERNS
12 WARNE
BIRDS' EGGS
18 WARNE
THE MILL ON THE FLOSS
A TALE OF TWO CITIES
INSECTS SHOWN TO THE CHILDREN
JACK

that we love and treasure, and few things on earth could be more meaningful than that. But what would it be like to create a space as portable and no-frills as Barbara's?

One of the reasons I love this home so much is because I haven't yet reached that stage in my life. Right now I'm too drawn to beautiful things, too invested in spending whatever free time I have combing antiques malls and flea markets, too addicted to the pleasure I get discovering something incredible at a really good price. At the same time, Barbara's interior reminds me that less can be more. Sometimes I wonder: *Would I appreciate the things around me more if I owned, say, one alligator picture frame instead of the three that currently sit on the table across from me?*

You won't find what Barbara has done in a design magazine or a website devoted to minimalism. The iconic interior she has put together may look easy to pull off, but believe me, it's not. Decades of experience, of comings and goings and beginnings and endings, and thinking and rethinking, have gone into the choices that determine what she has permitted into her home, and what she has chosen to leave behind. The stuff that remains is a pure, clear-eyed representation of exactly who Barbara Hill is. I'm pretty sure that if somehow I found myself sitting in her house, and she strode through the front door with a large crowd of people, I could pick her out in an instant. The hair, the cowboy boots, the jewelry, the dark glasses, the smile—they somehow belong with the concrete, steel, wood, and plaster. "That's you, right?" I would say. "And this is your house." And isn't recognizing yourself, and having other people recognize you for who you are, the goal of celebrating the things you live with?

STAND IN YOUR THRESHOLD
AND GUARD WHAT YOU ALLOW IN.

DOLORES ROBINSON

THERE AREN'T A WHOLE LOT OF PEOPLE whose entire lifetime is reflected in the things that surround them. And by *entire lifetime,* I mean the triumphs and the sorrows, the fat years and the lean years, the great vacations and the ones that got rained out, the babies, the politics, the poetry, the postcards, the tiny trinkets, the old books, the sweet friends, the days you couldn't wait to be done with, and the times you wanted to last forever. Because we're human, it's sometimes tempting to forget who we were way back when, and to edit our story and our stuff down so it celebrates only our successes.

Which is why on those occasions that I meet a woman who is so at ease and assured in her own skin, who has traveled so far, and whose stuff tells the truth, the whole truth, and nothing but the truth about that *entire* journey, it never fails to be an unforgettable experience.

This is a long way of saying that the only people who aren't madly in love with Dolores Robinson are ones who haven't had the privilege of meeting her, or the joy of visiting her lovely, light-filled home in Beverly Hills.

My first encounter with Dolores was in South Africa, during a party celebrating the opening of the Oprah Winfrey Leadership Academy for Girls. At the time, I had no idea that Dolores was a renowned Los Angeles talent manager, as well as the mother of actress Holly Robinson Peete, but I did know that I was in the presence of one of the warmest, smartest, sexiest, most authentic people I had ever met. All my life I've been drawn to strong, charismatic women—women who've figured out who they are and what they want, and have enough self-esteem to believe they deserve to get it. Needless to say, when Dolores told me she was in the process of renovating her house from head to toe, I was intrigued. Over the next few months, she emailed me questions about paint colors and what rug I thought should go where, and I was more than happy to give her a little advice. But she lives on one side of the country, and I live on the other, so I was left to wonder: How did that house finally turn out?

Just one glimpse of the great, weather-beaten U.S. Post Office bike standing in her driveway, its basket overflowing with blue-and-white hydrangea, and I feel like moving all my stuff into the guest bedroom, or at least dropping by Dolores's every Sunday afternoon for a glass of iced tea and a long conversation. That's the thing about Dolores's house: It may be in a canyon of Southern California, but it reminds everyone who visits of a house they love on the coast of Connecticut, or Massachusetts, or Maine. The interior may be "all about me feeling good," as Dolores says, but the fact is, her place makes everyone feel good. You walk in and can't help but feel like you've come home.

To truly understand what makes it so special, you first have to imagine the homes she was surrounded by as a 9-year-old girl growing up in Philadelphia, working alongside her mother, a housecleaner. Dolores would vacuum, dust, clean, and mop the upstairs of people's houses, while her mother did the downstairs. The upper-middle-class homes she worked in had long driveways, and fields where horses grazed behind white picket fences. Inside were hardwood floors, wainscoting, French doors, bead board, crown molding, and marble. Only when Dolores was halfway through decorating her Beverly Hills house did it dawn on her that she was re-creating the look and feel of the places she helped clean as a girl.

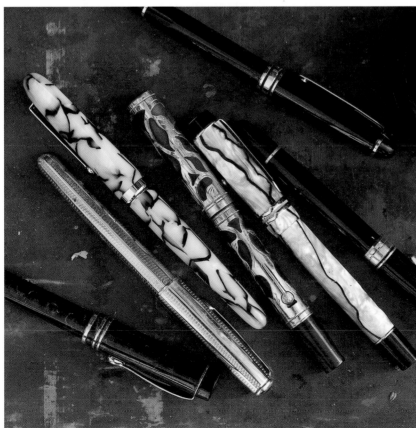

But Dolores also wanted to fill her home with mementos that have inspired her over the years and that continue to bring her joy. Things that connect her to her ancestors, her children, and her grandchildren. Not to mention all the people whose lives have intersected with hers, either personally or professionally. Barack Obama, who has unofficially adopted her as his "California mama," is on that list; Bill Clinton is also a friend, though he skips the formalities and just calls her "Mama"; and Ronald and Nancy Reagan used to invite her to their Santa Barbara ranch on the weekends. Even John F. Kennedy once picked her out of a huge crowd of supporters to point at her and wink.

"I'm just a girl with a dream," Dolores likes to say. In fact, when her home was finally finished, she lit a fire, brewed herself a cup of tea, and sent a photograph to all her friends with those words attached. If one of those dreams was to create the most welcoming living room in California, I'd say she's succeeded very well, thanks to the graceful white molding, a trayed ceiling, and beautiful French doors with antique latches that lead into the foyer and dining room. Overstuffed green-and-white-checked chairs surround the fireplace, whose andirons are hidden from view by a three-foot-high cardboard silhouette of a leopard, created by the pop artist Mo McDermott. If she's in the mood for a fire, the leopard obliges by relocating to the kitchen. Another piece by McDermott—a tall red palm tree silhouetted against the curtains—isn't going anywhere. Above the mantel, two wrought-iron warriors holding candlesticks flank a California plein air painting, while below, a rectangular glass coffee table showcases her collection of vintage magnifying glasses that she uses to peer into home and decorating magazines. Her favorite spot for that is in an old black leather chair she found on a Los Angeles street corner for $25. It may be losing a little of its stuffing, but that chair helps to create the perfect reading nook.

It's the three walls of books that make this living room feel so traditional and cozy. Novels and biographies share space with first-edition memoirs by friends Dolores has known since coming to Los Angeles in 1974. Mixed in with her book collection is an assortment of tiny snuff jars she found in Hong Kong antiques shops, and a collection of old baby shoes, including her children's and grandchildren's first slippers and sneakers, and, well, just some random baby shoes (Dolores has a thing for baby shoes). Above the shoes is a limited-edition faded purple six-pack of Snapple soda that her daughter Holly created when she was a finalist on *Celebrity Apprentice*. The soda, known as "Compassionberry Tea," was created and marketed in honor of her teenage grandson, R.J., who was born with autism. There's also plenty of Barack

Obama memorabilia, from bobble-headed dolls, to a vintage "Obama for Illinois Senator" yard sign, to a photograph of Dolores and the newly elected president, the former smiling that smile, the latter grinning that grin, the combined wattage of the two of them strong enough to light up the free world.

Then there's the desk, with attached inkwells on either side, which has a place of honor against the wall. It's hard to put into words how moved I am by this desk, or by the old family pictures in their vintage frames on top of it, including two shots of Dolores's grandfather, Reverend Jeremiah Lowe, who actually built this piece. If Dolores's grandchildren feel like digging a little deeper into family history, they can find more old photos inside a cracked leather-bound album. "I remember that desk from my childhood," Dolores says. "And I also remember standing on my tiptoes to look at those inkwells." The desk, with its attached hutch, is a jewel box, where Dolores keeps the things that matter most to her, ranging from a stack of miniature leather-bound Shakespeare plays to an assortment of vintage fountain pens that he loves simply because "those days are *over*—they don't make fountain pens like that anymore."

Hanging above the desk is a painting of a handsome young man in a hood, done by the artist Kehinde Wiley. Sharing the wall is Dolores's large collection of paintings and photographs of African Americans, including a vintage print titled *Negros Having Their Passes Checked on the Levees of New Orleans*, which a friend gave her right before Hurricane Katrina hit.

"I offend more people than you can imagine by referring to myself as 'just a little colored girl,'" Dolores says. "But, come on—I've got plenty of pride." Her lack of self-consciousness allows her to showcase the African American experience with a healthy mix of irreverence and matter-of-factness. After all, not a lot of black women would be secure enough in who they are to cover the walls of an entire bathroom in bright red Harlem Toile de Jouy, a fabric created by designer Sheila Bridges that, as Dolores says, "shows black people doing every stereotypical thing you can imagine, from playing basketball to eating fried chicken and watermelon." She has only one rule: If guests come out of the bathroom without laughing, she sends them right back in. For the record, she swears that if she ever sells the house to a Caucasian couple, she'll make a sign that reads, "We Didn't Put Up This Wallpaper—Blame the Black Lady Who Sold Us the Place."

I'm stopped cold by the old wooden washboard that hangs on the wall of Dolores's laundry room, with its top stamped "Columbus Washboard Co., Columbus, Ohio." It once belonged to her grandmother. Can you imagine all the hands that have touched it—that spent years of their lives scrubbing clothes clean on it? The washboard sits across the room from a sink, and a sign that reads, "Colored Women," while an old black woman in a bright red bandanna advertises "Fun-to-Wash Washing Powder." The evolution of how a family washboard ended up hanging in a Beverly Hills laundry room complete with two-inch-thick Carrera marble counters is almost impossible to fathom.

The plant-filled dining room is dominated by a spiky, dark green pineapple-shaped chandelier that hangs from a wrought-iron chain over the table, complementing the palm trees on a screen of French hand-blocked Zuber wallpaper. A Queen Anne mirror hangs above a primitive table that serves as Dolores's bar, while another table, this one with gold legs, plays host to a bucket plant. "R.J.—he's my grandchild with autism—loves this plant because it's carnivorous, so I keep it in here for him." The dining room chairs are slipcovered in simple white cotton. Most of the prints on the walls come from thrifting. One shows two old flower ladies sitting on a little country road in England, while another is a moody desert landscape. "I know I didn't pay more than $10 for any of these—I've just found them at various garage sales over the years," she says with a laugh. Then there are the bold, color-saturated, 1950s-era Haitian paintings of black people in court dress that hang in both the dining room and the foyer. They were a gift from an art dealer friend. "When I first traveled the world, one of the places I visited early on was Haiti," Dolores says. "I was kind of stunned by the political climate at the time, but I got to know and love that country, and those paintings always transport me."

A woven African bowl, filled with white bisque plaster pears, sits on the dining table, a souvenir from the night in South Africa when she and I first met. When we checked into our hotel, there was one in each room—a gift from Oprah. Attached to the basket was a card describing the number of people who had worked on the basket, how many hours it had taken them to do it, and how much they were paid. I'm glad Dolores still has hers, because I've still got mine.

But few things give Dolores more pleasure than her vast, airy kitchen, with its white molding, teal cabinets, and eleven-foot-long marble countertop, lined by six red-chrome 1950s-era stools—one for each grandchild. She even built her own baking closet, made from pinewood and overflowing with tins, cupcake baskets, mixers, rolling pins, and a Cuisinart, lit by a bare lightbulb with a single pull string attached to it that is vintage Grandma's house. If her grandkids would rather watch TV than perfect their pie-crust technique, they can head to the TV watching zone, with its pair of squishy white sofas, separated by a coffee table made out of two wicker doggie beds, where each of her Havanese likes to catch a nap.

An upright piano sits against the wall leading to the back of the house, decorated with a bust of Matthew Henson, the man who accompanied Admiral Peary to the North Pole in 1909 and a distant relative of Dolores's. Scattered around the kitchen and the back of the house are family Christmas cards she's sent to friends over the years; photos of her children and grandchildren (yes, that's her grown son, Matt, beaming beside a just-caught tuna); a poster advertising a children's book about autism, *My Brother Charlie*, written by Holly and her then-12-year-old daughter, Ryan; and mounted neon letters spelling out D-O-L-O-R-E-S. (It originally read "Happy 50th Birthday, Dolores," but the "Happy 50th Birthday" part was a rental, and the store needed it back.) At the base of one photo of her grandchildren is a scattering of miniature rocks. They come from the re-creation area at the Robben Island prison, a yard Nelson Mandela visited every day for eighteen years of his twenty-seven-year sentence.

The first thing you notice about Dolores's bedroom are the colored beads wrapped around the crystal chandelier. She strung them there last Christmas, and liked them so much she decided they should stay. Her dressing room is similarly homey, scattered with embroidered pillows that say things like "Ask Me About

My Grandchildren" and "What a Dump!", a photograph of Dolores with Oprah, and two chairs that were a gift from her old friend, singer Linda Ronstadt, where Dolores loves to curl up and read. A photo of her grandmother Lucinda looks down from one wall. "She used to tell me, 'You'll do all right in the world because you can look people in the eye,'" says her granddaughter, who meets Lucinda's gaze every morning.

A basket of red-and-pink knitting complements a hot pink lawn chair outside her bathroom. That's no coincidence, either. "The pink came from me getting breast cancer a few years ago," says Dolores, who is also the proud owner of two titanium knees. "Suddenly in this house, everywhere you looked, there was a touch of hot pink."

When Dolores wants a breath of fresh air, she can make her way outside, uncage Ike and Tina, her two enormous turtles, and plop down in her outdoor bedroom. You read that right. Pushed up against a stone wall, at the base of a hillside teeming with rosebushes and lavender, is a double bed complete with white sheets and a light blanket. A nearby fountain burbles, and a grill is ready to be lit if the day turns chilly. "When the sun goes down, it is just so heavenly," Dolores says. I agree, and if my New York apartment had a lawn, I'd be rolling out a bed faster than you can say "Whatever gets you through the night."

I've known many people from modest beginnings who succeeded in life beyond their wildest dreams, and God knows they're grateful for it. But not many of them are able to find harmony and balance and hop off the hamster wheel long enough to really grasp the meaning of "a life well lived." To me, it means surrounding yourself with the people and the pets and the things that bring you happiness every day. Dolores is one of those people who really gets that, and the proof is in how happy, and at home, her life makes everyone else feel.

"I'M JUST A GIRL WITH A DREAM."

CORIN NELSON

AlexPrager
The Big Valley · Week-end

I F THE PEOPLE I LOVE COME TO ME IN search of a good home-cooked meal, advice on child-rearing, an extra guy for a game of touch football, assistance in deciphering their tax returns, baiting a fishhook, or assembling a carburetor, I'm afraid they're out of luck. But there is one thing I definitely *can* do for a person I really care about, and that's help them make a home . . . even if they're not exactly looking for my help.

Corin Nelson is used to running the show—and she's got five Emmy Awards to prove she does it very well. What she didn't have when she left her apartment in Los Angeles for New York to sign on as executive producer of my talk show was a place to live. That was a major problem—not for Corin, who assured me she'd be fine staying in a hotel or a furnished corporate apartment, but for me.

It drives me crazy to see a friend trying to get by without beauty and comfort and at least a few tangible reminders of the things that really matter. I've always had a need to make sure my friends feel genuinely at home in their homes. And Corin Nelson isn't just a good television producer, she's also a good friend. Actually, for the two of us, it was love at first lunch. If Corin was going to serve as executive producer on my show, the chemistry had to be right because we'd be spending a lot of time together. There would be long days and exhausting nights, stomach bugs and head colds, last-minute script changes and bruised egos, cooking segments that go south and guests that go missing. There would be blizzards and lost luggage and pieces of furniture stuck on a truck somewhere in Buffalo, and the two of us would have to get through all of it, side by side. The first step would be to see if we could get through a Cobb salad and some conversation.

I didn't need to know about the work that Corin had done; her resume spoke for itself. What I wanted to find out was how she was going to treat the waiter and who she liked spending time with when she wasn't working. I wanted to know where she was coming from (both literally and figuratively) and why she wanted to be here with me instead.

This is what I found out: Corin grew up in New York, spending summers and weekends between houses in Montauk and Nantucket. She loved sailing and hiking and being at the beach with her sister, Shawn, and she still visits her mother at the cottage in Nantucket whenever she can. Corin also told me all about her mother's mother, Shirley Polykoff, the legendary copywriter who came up with iconic ad campaigns in the 1950s and '60s, such as "Blondes have more fun," "Does she or doesn't she?," and "Curlers in your hair . . . shame on you." Corin's grandmother was a businesswoman at a time when there weren't any, and she rose to number 24 on *Ad Age's* Top 100 People of the 20th Century list. They say that the Peggy Olsen character on *Mad Men* was based on Corin's grandmother. Her mom, Alix Frick, was an editor at Simon & Schuster who went on to have her own column in *The New York Times Book Review*.

A picture started to come into focus: Here was a grandmother, a mother, and a daughter, each with a deep love for their work, a clear understanding of popular culture, an eye on sales, and bestseller lists, shares, and rating points—three extraordinarily creative women who've lived their lives by the numbers.

After lunch, Corin and I headed to a little vintage clothing place on Prince Street. I'm not exactly sure how a job interview became a shopping expedition,

but what I was sure of was I liked her eye for detail, I liked her easy rapport with the salesperson, and I liked her laugh. There was only one thing I was worried about: "Won't you miss your home in Los Angeles?" I asked. Corin lifted the rose-gold charm necklace she was wearing and showed me a bird of paradise, its diamond-studded wings flying off to parts unknown. "LA is great, but my work is my passion," she explained. "So I've built a very mobile life for myself. I want to be free to take whatever job turns me on—even if that job happens to be 60 miles south of Timbuktu. Have passport and shoes, will travel!"

Over the next couple of months Corin worked nonstop, until I finally kidnapped her for a day of serious apartment-hunting, and we discovered a one-bedroom rental with high ceilings and a view of two things that she found irresistible: the Empire State Building and a hotel that's been around since the '20s. It wasn't the hotel itself that caught Corin's eye, but the red neon sign announcing its presence: the New Yorker. "Seeing this sign is a sign," she told me. "It's like I'm coming home." She was right; this was definitely a place Corin could call home. Well, at least by the time we got through with it.

It turns out my approach to design was a little bit different from hers. I believe in surrounding yourself with things you love. Corin believes you spend two weekends at Room & Board and you're pretty much set. "That's how I pulled my place in LA together, and it's been perfectly fine for me." I didn't doubt for a minute that Room & Board has good stuff and Corin has good taste, but I wanted my friend to have something more than "perfectly fine." I wanted to take care of her the way she takes care of everybody else.

I knew that the sofa and kitchen table she'd ordered were scheduled to be delivered, so my plan was to show up at the same time with a little surprise. First, let me backtrack: I'd been observing Corin since the day we met. I paid attention to how she dressed, which was mostly in black, gray, navy, and white, always with touches of chunky gold (think vintage Chanel) accessories mixed in. Her look reminded me of the way I'd always seen Parisians put themselves together; tailored, unobtrusive, chic. Other friends must've noticed the same thing, because two different people had given her coffee table books on French fashion as gifts.

I also studied the stuff that caught her eye whenever we'd window-shop together along the Lower East Side. Corin was drawn to nature and clean lines but she also had a rock & roll edge. I noted all of this while secretly accumulating a couple of shopping bags' worth of things that I thought would reflect her style and add a layer of history to her new apartment. On delivery day, bags in hand, I walked into her apartment, assuming I'd find my executive producer unpacking her fabulous kitchen table or sprawled across the sofa she'd chosen or plotting her next big furniture purchase. But the surprise was on me. Instead, I found the woman who has run multimillion-dollar productions, who's been responsible for managing a staff of 150 people, who's kept a bazillion parts all moving in the right direction, crying her eyes out.

"Work has always come first for me and I've always put home on hold." Corin's lips quivered and her nose ran. "But look at this! I mean, I actually bought a sofa that doesn't have any arms. Trying to make a home is just so, so . . ." She was stuck for a word, and then it hit her. "Personal." She wept some more. "I don't even know where to begin." I thought she should start by blowing her nose, but evidently she still had more melting down to do. "And," she sobbed, motioning toward a giant box, "my new kitchen table is almost twice the width of my new kitchen."

I looked at her in disbelief. I had seen this woman exhausted and exhilarated, I'd seen her resolute and reticent, I'd seen her organize and improvise, I'd seen her inscrutable, analytical, and occasionally cranky, but I'd never seen Corin Nelson vulnerable. "Are you kidding me?" I asked. I found her a Kleenex and told her to take a breath. And then I told her something I wished I'd said a little sooner: "I've got this."

Give a woman some stuff and she has some nice stuff for a while, but *teach* a woman how to find stuff that truly gets to the heart of who she is, and she's got a skill she can use to make herself feel at home for the rest of her life. Corin was

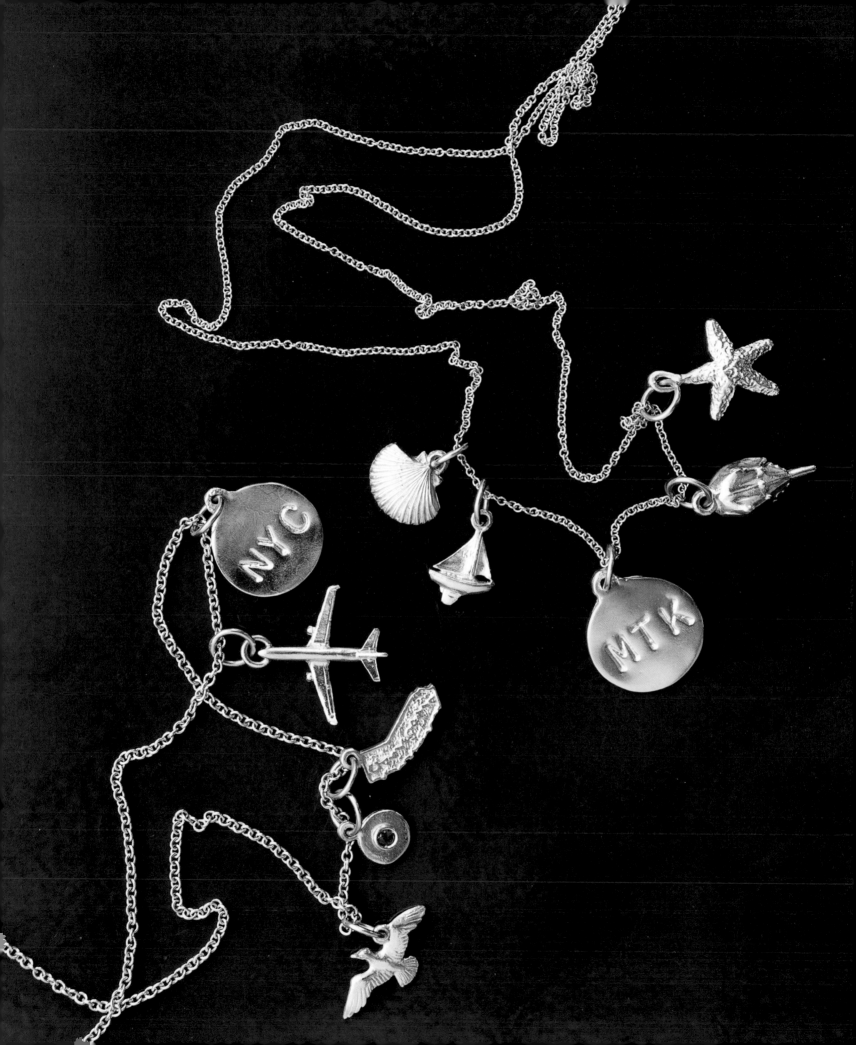

correct: Deciding on which things belong with you *is* deeply personal. I promised her that it wouldn't take long before this cold, white shell she was living in with nothing but a mattress and box spring, armless sofa, and giant table would be filled with intimacy and grace and a sense of permanence; that it would be warm and beautiful and everything else she is—that we were in this together. I wanted to show Corin how to find her way. I wanted her space to feel like a little jewel box in the sky—a concept that seemed as good a place as any to start.

"You have so many great pieces of jewelry," I said, remembering the charm necklace she wore the day we met. She told me she'd discovered the charms a few years earlier. "My stepfather had just passed away, I'd taken a brand-new job at MTV, and I was missing my family more than usual—which is saying something. Then I came across these charms: a starfish, a horseshoe crab, a scallop shell, a sailboat, and all kinds of other things that represent my roots. I wear them to stay connected to my memories. And I wear them whenever I'm attempting something new, something that might change the course of my life." She smiled and added, "I wore them to that first lunch of ours a few months ago."

"So, wouldn't it make you happy to be able to see those charms even when you're not wearing them?" I asked. The question dovetails into Corin's first assignment: "I want you to go out this weekend and find three or four glass boxes that we can use to display some of your favorite pieces of jewelry," I said. Three days later, I received an email. It was Corin sending a picture and seeking my approval on three glass boxes, all in different sizes, all perfect for her windowsill, her bookcase, and her bedroom. Those boxes instantly had my blessing. Because Corin is an outdoors girl, I didn't hesitate to pick up the two small white porcelain bowls that I found at a neighborhood thrift shop. Each bowl was decorated with a bumblebee and signed by Boehm. They now hold her charm necklace and the bird of paradise in mid-flight.

Knowing that Corin was heading for a few days of R&R in Los Angeles, I studied pictures of her apartment there and asked her to pack up a few things and bring them back to Manhattan. "I want you to have your favorite shoes here; they'll make you feel good every time you open your closet. And what are those pictures hanging over your desk? Bring 'em!" I said. "I want you to have photographs of the people you love and the places that make you happiest. I want you to revisit everyone and everything when you look at them." Corin told me that her sister, Shawn, makes beautiful tableware and wrapping paper. She wasn't kidding. The plates I saw in

those pictures were pared-down, sophisticated, and very reminiscent of a New England summer. "I want her on the show! And I want you to pack some plates, too—we'll hang them over the sofa. And while you're doing all that," I said, "I'm going to be doing some furniture shopping in Florida."

Sometimes even the most unlikely spots are filled with buried treasure. There's a strip mall in Hollywood, Florida, that is home to a warehouse most people would pass right by, but I've yet to leave that place without hitting the mother lode. I found Corin a night table with an ivory inlay, circa 1965, in that place. It looks exactly like one she'd admired when we were window-shopping on Ludlow Street. I also found a French vintage coffee table with a fantastic gold base. I wasn't crazy about the top but I knew the table would be great, just as soon as Corin had a new piece of glass with a one-inch overlay cut to replace it. I also found a little gold bench with a padded cushion for her entryway. It was your basic mess, but nothing that a quick reupholstering wouldn't take care of. Next I found a pair of Louis XVI–style chairs that I'll be the first to admit were not pretty—but when I look at old pieces I see what could be, and it was obvious to me that these two chairs could be extraordinary, despite their worn olive-green velvet fabric and hideous walnut arms and legs. This was not quite as obvious to Corin, who was somewhat less than bowled over by the photo I sent. She texted back one word: *blecchhh!*

Corin's response to the Florida finds wasn't much better when she saw them in person. "Seriously?" she said after circling the little gold bench several times. I went straight to the phone and called the show's art department. "Can somebody go through our fabric remnants, pull out anything in navy, black, white, and gray"— we decided to base the palette for her apartment on the clothing colors she favors— "and run it over to Corin's place?" One hour later, Corin claims I switched into MacGyver mode. She swears there were pliers and bobby pins and I-don't-even-know-what involved, but really, I just popped the seat out, and stapled a black-and-gray print over the existing material. Now it looks like a very expensive piece where she can sit and put her shoes on before running out the door in the morning. As for the two green-velvet chairs that Corin dubbed "Viva Las Vegas meets my grandparents," well, I had the wood painted in a high-gloss white and the cushions reupholstered in a Dior-like gray linen. They are now something she intends to have and to hold until death does them part.

Then it was time for Corin to show me what she'd brought back from her Los Angeles trip. She'd returned with the three timeless black-and-white portraits I'd noticed hanging above her desk in LA: one of her grandmother, one of her mother, and one of her sister and herself as toddlers. "The frames can all stay different, like they are now, but we'll get white mats cut so they feel unified," I tell her. Next came a sepia-toned shot of a charming little village. "Italy is my favorite place in the world, which is why I've gone on seven bike trips there in the last ten years." Corin's voice takes on a dreamy quality. "Alberobello is surrounded by olive groves—and I really don't think it's changed much from the twelfth century, when it was designed by . . . well, my guess is it was designed by Keebler elves," she said. "No matter how stressed-out I get, I look at that photo and I know there's this little place on the other side of the world and it reminds me that the world is filled with infinite possibility, and I exhale." I make a note to reframe the picture in something that echoes its serene mood.

The infamous armless sofa got pillows from the Nate Berkus Collection. I designed the gold pouf, too; it was sitting in my office but I thought it would be much happier as extra seating in Corin's living room. I wanted my friend to have a reading area, too, so I loaned her my Milo Baughman chaise from the 1970s. It couldn't be more comfortable, and nothing makes me smile like the thought of Corin lounging on it after an intense stretch at work. Her plates are hung as planned, above the sofa. Also above the sofa is a piece of Asian fabric, navy blue with two slightly lighter blue footprints in the center. I found it in a gallery in Venice Beach, California; it felt like a good mix of New York urban and Southern California cool. Corin spotted a white ceramic bowl with a blue-green interior for the bookcase. It reminded us of a bird's nest, so she filled it with two flawless marble eggs. If all it takes is love and warmth, I'm sure that sooner or later those eggs are bound to hatch. Finally, a gray-and-white-striped dhurrie rug ordered from a website galvanizes the living room.

With each new addition, Corin got more and more into the spirit of bonding her story to her stuff. She also gained some confidence in her choices and recognizing what she calls the "infinite possibilities" of her home. She even fell madly in love with an Alex Prager photograph and bought it immediately. The piece, *Wrath*, is a gritty, exhilarating shot of a woman in mid-tantrum. I think Corin finds it cathartic. "Remember those scenes in *Broadcast News* when Holly Hunter would just unplug her phone for ninety seconds, have a mini freak-out, and then get back to work? Producers need a little primal scream at the end of the day . . . just to get themselves ready for the next day," she said. "So when I discovered this lady in blue letting go for a minute, I decided to bring her home with me, so that there'd always be somebody around who understands."

When it was time for us to talk about the living room, Corin told me we needed to have a different kind of talk first. "You better sit down," she said. She looked solemn and kind of nervous. I'm thinking someone has died while I was hanging dishes and breaking down boxes. "Nate," she said. "I read up on you before we actually met, and there was this interview you gave where you said something that I found . . . unsettling. Well, maybe not unsettling, exactly—it was more, uhm . . ." She started to stammer and I was starting to panic. "WHAT DID I SAY?" I shouted. She finally came out with it. "You said you thought that the TV shouldn't be in the living room because then it becomes the focal point and the living room should be about friends and family and actual living. Nate," she pleaded, "I *need* my TV in here." Once we'd established that everybody was still breathing, I explained that I stood by my statement, but I was speaking in general. "Your home is about who *you* are, and you, my friend, are a television producer. TV is important to you and you should have it where you'll enjoy it the most." I think it's safe to say we were both extremely relieved.

For the bedroom. Corin found a simple white bed with two big built-in storage drawers that looked great next to that 1960s nightstand I had shipped back from Florida. We both flipped for a lamp with a rough, earthy, insanely heavy concrete base and we put it on the nightstand, partly because it looked good there and partly because nobody felt like lifting it again. I also handed Corin one more thing to keep beside her bed: "This journal is for you," I said, "so if inspiration hits in the middle of the night, and you come up with an idea for any future projects we can work on together, you get to jot it down, right then and there." Needless to say, I've been encouraging her to sleep late and dream big ever since.

We also added a lamp from my collection to a small white dresser by the window; its shade is a textured charcoal gray linen, and a reflection of the entire room shines in its mercury glass base. But my favorite thing in Corin's bedroom is the two panels of vintage wallpaper that hang in their original bamboo frames above the bed. I saw them while surfing on One King's Lane and I couldn't believe it. They were navy and white, preppy and free-spirited, a little bit no-nonsense and a little bit feminine. They were modern but they had a history. They were Corin to the core. I emailed the picture with a two-word message, "Buy them!" Corin emailed back, "Very nice. Let me think about it." Clearly my two-word message needed ten additional words: "Buy them before somebody else does and I'm forced to kill you!" Corin now loves them even more than I do. "I'm not exactly sure why," she said the other day, "but they actually seem to double the size of the bedroom."

"My work here is officially done," I told Corin one day after arranging a vintage necklace, a couple of books, and a very pretty box covered in white shells on her coffee table. "Wait!" said my friend, going into the closet and reaching for a shopping bag. "I walked into this store when I was in California, and I saw a very special thing that I'm pretty sure belongs in here." She handed me something that looked like a river stone, smooth and oval. "It's actually made of iron, by a Japanese artist," she said. I felt something weighty inside, and it made a soft sound when I gave it a gentle shake. Corin explained that the artist collects shards of gravel and sand from his motorcycle travels through the mountains, fills each iron stone with it, and then welds the piece closed. This struck me as a perfect melding of sleek, contemporary sculpture and raw nature. "Wow!" I said. "You found this incredible expression of who you are and it's amazing." Corin asked me if I was just being charitable or if I really loved it. I have faked my way through many a mediocre dinner, and I've kept quiet when somebody gets a haircut I'm not completely crazy about, but I'd never claim to love a design if I didn't. "It's beautiful," I told her. "Good," Corin answered, going back into her shopping bag, "because I brought one home for you, too!"

Corin Nelson will always be a wanderer, but at the end of this particular leg of her journey, she has a *real* home to return to. And whether it remains a high-rise in Manhattan, or eventually turns out to be a beach house in Santa Monica, a cottage in Nantucket, or a hut 60 miles south of Timbuktu, she now has things that tell the story of a life filled with bike rides through Italy, summers spent beachcombing along the Eastern seaboard, charms that see her through every life-changing event, and three striking portraits of strong, smart women whose legacy she is more than living up to.

"TRYING TO MAKE A HOME IS JUST SO, SO...PERSONAL."

FABIOLA BERACASA

"As human beings, our greatness lies not so much in being able to remake the world... as in being able to remake ourselves."
- Gandhi

I ♥ BALI DOGS
SAYA PEDULI DENGAN ANJING BALI

OFFICIAL NEW YORK STATE PRESCRIPTION
ROBERT M. LERCH MD
2 FIFTH AVENUE NEW YORK, NY 10011 (212) 473-6497
934 MANHATTAN AVE. BROOKLYN, NY 11222 (718) 389-8585

Patient Name   Jack Doughty
Address
City   State   Zip   Age   Sex M/F
Rx
                Patient is cool
                even when he
                doesn't drink

RICCARDO TISCI

Dear Fabiola,
You looked beautiful at the MET,
can't wait to see you again!
Love,

Dear Fabiola,
We wish you an
Amazing beautiful
New Year to come,

May
Holiday S...
blessed...

Tatiana

Transforma
PAUL

"La Guérite"

TIME 1...
...to issue we name the...
LEA...
Luiz In...
J. T. Wa...
Admiral M...
Barack Ob...
Ron Bloom
Yukio Hatoya...
Dominique Stra...
Nancy Pelosi
Sarah Palin
Salam Fayyad
Jon Kyl
Glenn Beck
Annise Parker
Tidjane Thiam
Jenny Beth Martin
Christine Lagarde
Recep Tayyip Erdogan
General Stanley McChrystal
Manmohan Singh
Bo Xilai
Mark Carney
Sister Carol Keehan
Sheik Khalifa bin Zayed al-Nahyan
Robin Li
Scott Brown
HEROES
Bill Clinton
Kim Yu-Na
Mir-Hossein Mousavi
Ben Stiller

BACK IN THE EARLY 1980S, WHEN I WAS in middle school, we used to spend entire afternoons carefully cutting out pictures of friends and gluing them into collages on a big piece of colored cardboard. And if, like me, you were lucky enough to have a mother who was willing to drive you to Target so you could buy an actual picture frame, you could even mount that photo board behind glass and hang it on your bedroom wall to enjoy when you weren't busy enjoying things like Pac-Man and *Dynasty* and New Cokc.

I'm not sure when it was decided that these photo boards of people laughing, kissing, flashing a peace sign at the camera, and just plain acting goofy should be packed away, along with our "We Are the World" T-shirts and Blondie LPs, but I was really sorry to see them go.

Fabiola Beracasa is the last person on earth (aside from maybe Kim Jong-un and the pope) you'd expect to have picture boards in her home, but it's probably one of the things I like best about my friend. One of the most sophisticated, worldly women I know, Fab was born in Venezuela, but moved to the Upper East Side of New York City when she was 5 years old and her mother, Veronica, married the late Randolph Hearst. Fabiola went to boarding school in Switzerland, interned for Karl Lagerfeld and Chanel in Paris, and today works for a downtown art gallery and as a contributing editor for *Elle* and *Interview* magazines. She's a smart, sensitive, passionate, hardworking, one-of a-kind woman, and all of this shines through in her home. Her Greenwich Village penthouse duplex reflects a life in perpetual motion.

Fabiola may be a regular on Manhattan's social scene, but inside this bohemian, darkly romantic person is an 11-year-old kid alone in her room, scissoring out the silhouettes of her favorite people and sticking them onto sheets of colored cardboard. One of her two photo boards rests against the wall just off her downstairs sitting area, across from a swatch of daffodil-yellow flocked wallpaper; the second sits at the foot of her tub, so she can see it while she's soaking.

When I was growing up, my mom didn't allow us to eat sugary breakfast cereal. Needless to say, as soon as I got to boarding school in Massachusetts, I proceeded to wolf down about forty-three pounds of Lucky Charms a day—for breakfast, lunch, and dinner. The truth is, there are still times when I'd take a bowl of Cap'n Crunch over a four-star meal.

My point is that when you're born to a household of rules and, in Fabiola's case, from a background that stresses manners and traditions, it seems to me you've got two options: You can become a slave to what you were taught, or your upbringing can create the very foundation that allows you to experiment and take risks. There are people who thumb their nose at tradition because they couldn't care less, and then there are people who have learned the rules by heart, and respect them, even love them, but feel free to break every single one of them.

Fabiola belongs in the second category. "I'm not the sort of person who buys the latest L-shaped couch, or who spends her days leafing through a cutting-edge design magazine," she says. If an object pleases her, she doesn't care

what other people think about it. "I try to fill my home with things I genuinely like, and not because I should like them." My friend understands that decorating is about having a good time, and surrounding yourself with things—in her case, amethyst bangles, plastic flowers, decadent dishes, and whatever else strikes her fancy—whose only purpose is to delight her.

For this reason, Fabiola has filled her home with stuff she adores, ranging from antique English chairs and heirloom rugs, to exotic objects and sculptures from her travels in the Far East, to contemporary art from the gallery where she works, to flea market finds, to pieces she's salvaged from her parents' and grandparents' cellars and attics. Throw in a slice of red velvet cake, or one of the cookies she keeps out on her kitchen counter for friends who drop by, and you have a quirky, iconic space that can't help but charm anybody who walks through the front door.

In her upstairs sitting room, a sculpture of orange-and-yellow butterflies delicately placed on a branch inside a glass canister sits on a vintage tray on top of a black age-worn Chinese table—a gift from Fabiola's father. The table is flanked by two red-and-white English chairs, while on a sideboard a white ceramic puppy by the artist Jeff Koons stands guard over a stack of magazines, beside a broken tree branch ("It was a dowsing stick, one of those sticks that finds water," Fabiola says wistfully, "or at least so I dreamed it to be."). Family china that Fabiola mounted on a living room wall shares space with a wildly colorful sculpture created by a contemporary artist named Dear Raindrop. "I just call it 'The Piece,'" Fabiola says. "Every time I look at it, something pops out at me that I've never seen before." Five miniature Persian wall prints she inherited from her grandmother overlook a set of vintage red bar stools she found at a flea market. Friends have offered to polish up the chrome, but Fabiola absolutely refuses.

She has softened the edges of the modern, triangular space by installing a comfortable, pillow-filled window seat around her dining room table, and adding vintage light fixtures. The glass dining room table balances on three tall exotic drums. "I was part of a drum circle in college," Fabiola says. "I loved my drums, so instead of throwing them away, or putting them in storage, I leveled them off and use them as my table base."

Above the table are two unframed Eddie Martinez paintings. Something about the lack of frames makes the beauty of these two pieces come alive, and I can't take my eyes off of them. But it's what's underneath the paintings that never fails to thrill me: a pair of heirloom gold candlesticks (think Versailles!) that Fabiola's

mother gave her, dripping over with a frozen fountain of dark red candle wax. Only a rebellious spirit would be brazen enough to leave red wax all over the table, to find it beautiful and even kind of sexy—which, believe me, it is. "Candle wax is about talking and friendship and fun and late nights," says Fabiola, adding, "I scrape it off when it starts to get dusty." The table has another amazing piece on it: a circular glass bowl with an indentation of two cupped hands at its base. The only problem, as Fabiola says, is that when you actually place anything in the bowl, like flowers, the glass hands are concealed. "Sometimes I'll put a couple of green M&M's in there," she says with a laugh.

Beside the door that leads to the terrace—where a heavy wooden Balinese couch shares space with four pink flea market chairs—is a small chalkboard. Every time Fabiola has friends over, she writes out their names, as well as what she's planning to serve. And when they're done eating, they can take turns sitting in Fabiola's red beaded African King's chair that she bought at a Manhattan flea market.

Five black-and-white Helmut Newton nudes strike a pose as you descend the stairwell into an art-and-book-filled sitting room. Fabiola's goal was to create a sanctuary from the honk and hustle of the city and, again, to soften the concrete

modernity of her apartment. "I wanted this room to feel like windows to the sky," she says. The sitting area does make it seem like you're drifting across the cosmos, thanks to three dark-green-and-turquoise paintings of clouds and sky. A glass terrarium of ferns rests on a black-and-white Moroccan table she found in a Manhattan antiques store; it's surrounded by four overstuffed club chairs (she salvaged them from her family's attic, then re-covered them in red).

The bookshelves are made from knotty reclaimed wood Fabiola came across in an upstate New York barn. They spill over with books, photographs, a ukulele, a big china bulldog, a vintage alarm clock, and additional souvenirs from her travels overseas. Other books devoted to fashion and design perch like mini art installations at the bottom of the stairs and along the hallway that leads to her bedroom. Then there's the bamboo chair hanging from the ceiling chain underneath the eave of the stairwell. Fabiola likes to dangle there and read from time to time.

When she's not cocooned in the sitting room, she's usually tucked away in her cozy guest bedroom, a room she says was inspired by her grandmother, a patroness of the arts who kept a similar spot in her house, to host young visiting

artists and musicians. A daybed covered with tartan throws and pillows sits on a black-and-white wool rug. Behind the couch is a wall covered with prints from all eras and cultures, dominated by a huge round mirror whose original gold leaf Fabiola repainted black, as well as a centuries-old piece of fabric she bought from an antiques collector in Thailand and hung in an ornate gold frame. Leave it to Fabiola to decide that what works best with a piece of ancient Thai fabric is a totally contemporary flowerpot sculpted entirely out of spray cans. The juxtaposition makes both things look even more extraordinary. A small television sits across from the bed, not that anyone would ever know it, as the screen is covered with a playful, hand-woven Peruvian fabric of two tigers. "I have a pet peeve about TVs," Fabiola says.

"My mother would always tell me, 'You don't photograph your bedroom,'" Fabiola says. Clearly the advice didn't take, since she leads me into the calm, shadowed room where she sleeps. In search of a nontraditional place to lay her head, she found a Balinese canopied bed that reminds her of the antique four-poster she slept in as a child. The wood, the teak, the height, the carvings on the headboard, and the white silken sashes all say "exotic, mysterious, ultra-feminine"— but the I ♥ pillow says "girl with a BlackBerry." There is no bedside table, no stack of books, no reading lamp. "I like all that stuff to be hidden," she says.

More than any other space in the apartment, Fabiola loves her dressing room. "I mean, *c'mon,*" she says. I see what she's talking about. The place is like a grotto, or a rain forest, or the perfect getaway. You almost expect an old Gypsy woman to appear from the shadows with a finger pressed to her lips. The first thing you see is a large figurine of a gray cat hanging over the antique French writing desk Fabiola has converted into a makeup table. On second glance, it could be a lion, or a puma, but it doesn't really matter. Ringed by fur, it looks up with a surprised, fairly fierce expression. The cat, which Fabiola bought from a student artist, oversees the beads, belts, and bangles that seem to drip from everywhere. Jackets and blouses tilt out suggestively from the closets, while inside are drawers devoted to scarves, dark glasses, handbags, bracelets, brooches, and some of the most fantastic rings I've ever seen.

Fabiola's mirror is covered with a piece of black lace. Beside it stands a vintage lamp with no lamp shade whose squiggly, old-school lightbulb was found in a vintage lighting store; and a lorgnette made of chocolate (the woman has chocolate opera glasses) sits amid half a dozen perfume bottles on an antique tray. Hanging against the wall is a chalkboard that she uses to scrawl messages to herself, some of them real, some of them made up, including "Lunch with Grace Jones" and "Must reply to Mick Jagger" and, my personal favorite, "Call Prince Charles back—again!"

I keep returning to the two photo boards, and not only because I happen to be in one of them. For reasons I can't quite fathom, let alone explain, in one of the photos I'm sinking my teeth into someone's foot. I have absolutely no memory of where that picture was taken, but my guess is there was a fair amount of tequila involved. Can I just say again what a lack of self-consciousness it takes not only to

exhibit a photo board, but to position the thing at the foot of your bathtub, adjacent to a large painting showing an oversized Mickey Mouse being terrorized by real white mice? "I've been making photo boards since I was a kid," Fabiola says. "You can see the progression of life and sometimes even love." She closes her eyes and is momentarily transported. "It feels almost like a relic from another time."

I think she's right. I also think that years from now, Fabiola's interior will be remembered, celebrated, and loved as much as I love it today. Why? Because she allows candle wax to drip and drip on her dining room table, and because she hangs mesmerizing paintings without frames above that table, and because she stacks her art and fashion and design books on her hallway floors. Because she combines mid-century caned chairs with an incredible piece of modern art with Persian miniature prints and a red beaded African King's chair and the most delicious red velvet cake I've ever tasted. Because she makes no apologies for who she is, and what brings her joy. If our spaces are made up of a symphony of voices that come together to create the music we love living with, Fabiola has found a wild melody.

THERE ARE PEOPLE WHO HAVE LEARNED
THE RULES BY HEART, AND RESPECT THEM,
EVEN LOVE THEM, BUT FEEL FREE TO
BREAK EVERY SINGLE ONE OF THEM.

SANDY FOSTER

I T'S RARE THAT I COME ACROSS SOMEONE whose design style is so clear, and whose palette is so succinct, that I find myself marveling at the clarity of that person's space. I mean, you can't help but be charmed by a home so compact and unified that by merely floating three branches of green hydrangea in a bowl on the mantelpiece, or laying out a handful of orangey-red leaves, or plugging in a cord of small white holiday bulbs, its owner serves notice that the seasons have changed from spring to summer, summer to fall, and fall to winter. On top of a steep hill in the Catskills, Sandy Foster has created that place, an ethereal, harmonious dreamscape where time stands so still you can practically hear the flowers growing.

MANY OF US HAVE A MOMENT WHEN WE REALIZE WE'RE WAITING FOR OUR LIVES TO BEGIN. . . . WHAT ARE WE WAITING FOR?

What I love so much about this space isn't just what Sandy did, it's what she *didn't* do. From the four exterior porch columns to the peeling hunter-green front door, to the raw industrial legs of a table salvaged from the side of a country road, Sandy has thought a lot about every design choice both inside and outside her 400-square-foot fantasy getaway. And though it's taken some time and research and serious bargain hunting, by surrounding herself with what she wants, Sandy is at long last getting what she needs.

The interior space is a mix of curbside and flea market finds, Victorian mirrors, and objects Sandy just plain loves. The house may be a study in white, but its textures, from intricate lace to chipped paint to unfinished wood, keep things interesting. Anchoring the cottage is a white love seat filled with puffed-up pillows in chamois-soft cases. A metal chandelier strung with crystal beads hangs from the ceiling, its chain swathed in white linen (courtesy of an old shirt that Sandy cut up, sewed together again, and scrunched over the chain). Against the far wall are old French doors, behind which are scattered, among other things, Christmas ornaments and design magazines bundled in twine. To my right, a white table stands on its original rusted sawmill legs, holding half a dozen folded white linens. The nearly seven-foot-tall ceiling is made from vintage pieces of stamped tin that Sandy repainted white. Mirrors hang and tilt from every wall, and if you stand on your tiptoes, you see a white sleeping loft that would go perfectly with a cup of chamomile tea and a good bodice ripper.

Many of us have a moment when we realize we're waiting for our lives to begin. And that always makes me wonder: What are we waiting for? We keep our best plates and stemware out of sight, hidden in a hutch, or tucked away in a buffet. We figure that one of these days we'll have a special occasion or we'll throw a big

party and they'll be great. But all that fine china ends up staying put. Along with the matching silver. That serving set we inherited from our great-grandmother? It might break. So we stick with our everyday stuff, when only a few feet away the plates and bowls and glasses and forks and knives and spoons are on standby, waiting to become part of the life that, for one reason or another, we're just not giving ourselves permission to live.

Sandy remembers what finally shook her awake. It was 2008, the year she began thinking seriously about building her own house. Since college, she'd been collecting good china at flea markets. One Saturday afternoon she finally decided to sit down and unwrap her plates, only to see that the newspaper she was using to protect them was dated 1996. Let's think about this: In 1996, rebels were fighting Russian soldiers in Chechnya, Tom Cruise was showing Cuba Gooding Jr. the money in *Jerry Maguire,* and Sandy Foster was storing away all the stuff that brought her pleasure for what would turn out to be twelve long years. "It took me until 2008 to actually use that china," Sandy says with a sigh. "Up until that moment, I was waiting for the day when someone would step in and help me lead the life I had going on in my head."

Sandy had had that picture-perfect life in her head ever since she was a kid. Growing up in a treeless Long Island suburb of cookie-cutter houses, she was always drawn to old things, particularly the graceful, character-filled turn-of-the-century architecture of her grandparents' house in Detroit. But grace was in short supply during Sandy's adolescence. Her father, a radio announcer, had substance abuse issues, and was often out of work. One day, Sandy, a high school honors student, came home to find her family being evicted from their house. A week later, her parents had put most of their belongings in storage, bought a tent, and begun moving from one state park to the next.

Sandy told no one, even though her family's homelessness was staring everybody in the face, and there were many nights spent in sleeping bags on the floor of a friend's basement. A few years later, after completing college (thanks to a whole lot of student loans), Sandy realized that what she craved more than anything else was stability, a nest where she could feel safe.

Despite its miniature proportions, Sandy's cottage is surprisingly airy. The illusion of space is helped by countless mirrors, among them a French rococo-style floor-to-ceiling mirror from the 1920s that she picked up at a yard sale for $22. The mirror was originally the color of a Band-Aid, but Sandy painted it white,

and then distressed it, though the beautiful ghosted, beveled glass speaks for itself. Hanging off the mirror are a fragile pair of angel wings that Sandy made out of baling wire she bought at a tractor supply store, and then tarnished.

She decorated her mantel with a $2 bowl, and it looks as perfect sitting there as anything at Baccarat could. Her billowing white curtains come from Target (total cost: less than $25), and are attached to the window frames with clear pushpins. She chose to leave some sawhorse legs, as well as a door she rescued from another house, unfinished, because they cut through what she calls "the saccharine sweetness" of her girlish style. For the record, I like them this way, too. I also like that she's bold enough to showcase a sculptural-looking tree branch because she realizes that at the end of the day nature is really a pretty hard thing to improve on.

Think about the joy we get from surrounding ourselves with stuff that is well loved, maybe a little dog-eared, or even altogether imperfect; stuff that we've shared over the years with friends and family. Imagine putting your hand on a doorknob that's been around for 150 years, versus, say, a gleaming new one that makes a little clicking sound when you turn it. Are there pieces in your home that sing a little song to you every time you walk by, things you love to touch, things that instantly transport you to a different time and place, things that knit you into the world in some way?

Sandy has this connection to everything in her tiny house, whether it's a dried-out fish vertebrae she found on the beach, a set of antique wine tumblers lined up against a windowsill, or the wirework baskets she's taken to collecting. Her latest discovery is a church candlestick inspired by a design trend that's popular across Scandinavia. Bypassing the $500 it would cost to buy a new one, and with the help of heavy wire clippers and tin-cutting scissors, she sliced flowers, leaves, and grapes out of scrap tin, then wrapped everything tight with 22-gauge wire. The candlestick, known in Denmark as a *"kirkenstagel,"* sits proudly on the white, blistered-wood mantelpiece.

The back of the room is entirely given over to a pyramid of books, magazines, and Sandy's collection of Limoges china, sitting behind a protective screen made out of chicken wire that she spray-painted white and attached to the wall with a staple gun. She created the bookshelves using scrap pieces of floor from the renovation of an old farmhouse. Book spines aren't uniform in color or size or font, so in an effort to maintain her tranquil palette, she created slipcovers out of thick gray paper for each volume in her library, as well as gray magazine cases that outfit her collections of old home decorating magazines.

Above the room, accessible only by a ladder, is that small sleeping loft, which she insulated herself. It is by far her favorite spot in the house, and I can see why. The place is just big enough for two people to curl up. "I feel like a kid in a tree house up here," she tells me. What look like curtains flowing from the ceiling around either side of the loft are in fact nothing more than panels of sheer white paper. Beginning in October, Sandy says, it starts to get blustery outside. An electric space heater cuts the cold, but in November, when the snow begins falling, she brings in a propane-fired heater with an electrical wire that snakes across the creek and into the trailer she shares with her husband, Todd. Someday, she says, she'd like to build a fireplace or, at the very least, install a woodstove.

For now, she relishes her private hangout. She reads, she blogs (My Shabby Streamside Studio has nearly one million hits, to date), she takes photographs and gardens; she listens to Neil Young, the Beatles, and her all-time favorite band, Rush; and she plays with Zuzu, her Maltese, who, fortunately for all parties concerned, is creamy white and therefore does not require a slipcover.

A lot of us daydream about a space where we could sit for hours, gazing out at a stream, or at wildflowers, where we could read or write or play our music as loud as we want to with nobody yelling at us to turn it down. Sandy Foster has gone the extra mile and actually built that fantasy space for herself, and she's done it with little more than some practical magic, perseverance, an unerring eye for detail, and an authentically romantic spirit.

"I FEEL LIKE A KID IN
A TREE HOUSE UP HERE."

BROOKE & MICHAEL HAINEY

W HEN YOU'VE GOT FOUR BROTHERS and a sister, you figure out pretty early on that being an introvert just doesn't work. As a result, I never really hesitate to grab a microphone, stand in front of a large group of people, and say whatever needs saying. But when it came time to toast my friends Brooke Cundiff and Michael Hainey at their wedding reception in New York last year, I got up, raised my glass, and proceeded to dissolve into tears.

I cried because I'm so impressed with the way these two very different people have learned to allow for each other's differences. I cried because I'm so inspired by the way they always seem to have each other's backs, nourish each other's creativity, and genuinely enjoy hanging out together. And I cried because in a world where love can be pretty elusive, Michael and Brooke actually found each other—even though they had to travel to another continent to do it.

They were both in Milan on business. Michael is an artist, author, and the deputy editor of *GQ*. Brooke is now vice president of brand relations/fashion director for Park & Bond and Gilt Groupe, but in those days she was working as a buyer and living in Chicago. They kept spotting each other across the runways of various fashion shows. Season after season, Michael would casually sneak a peek at Brooke when she wasn't looking, and season after season, Brooke would be as nonchalant as possible while checking Michael out whenever she thought she could get away with it. Then, one evening, they found themselves at the same noisy, crowded party, and Brooke, being very resourceful, managed to "accidentally" bump straight into Michael. People bump into me at parties all the time, they spill their red wine, they step on my foot, and it's never once ended in us deciding to have and to hold until death do us part, but Brooke and Michael always go that extra mile.

Actually, Brooke went hundreds of miles. She'd grown restless in Chicago, and finally decided to make the move to Manhattan. It wasn't long before her friendship with Michael turned to love and love led to a one-bedroom, prewar, Greenwich Village apartment where the two of them could merge their lives, to say nothing of their families, their friends, and, of course, their stuff. But how exactly do two very distinct personalities with very distinct ideas about how to live in a space go about doing that? The friends-and-family thing I get; you make the introductions, stand back, and hope for the best. But the commingling of stuff is a whole other challenge.

Brooke and I were neighbors in Chicago before we were neighbors in New York. When I first met her, I took one look at this tall, thin, beautiful blonde and made certain assumptions. I assumed she'd be icy. I assumed she'd be a snob. I assumed she'd be one of those rigidly organized girls who was born with perfect hair, straight teeth, and all of her homework done. In reality, my thin, blond friend is one of the sweetest, most down-to-earth people I know. She abhors gossip, she has no agenda, she's got a really bawdy sense of humor, and she's unbelievably loyal. As for her intense need to keep every surface clutter-free to within an inch of its life . . . let's just say it takes a neat freak to know a neat freak. Brooke's style was always very done, very elegant, and, like my own, immaculately organized.

Michael, on the other hand, is what we fastidious types call "normal." I'm told that normal people like to relax a little and spread out occasionally. They've got some paperwork on their desks and maybe even a couple of

notebooks. They believe in throwing a wild card into the mix every now and then. That's Mike. He jots down shards of poetry, and ideas for paintings, he collects quotes that move him and pictures that provoke an emotion, he improvises, he takes chances, he embraces whimsy, he pays attention to the details.

So with Michael living the informal life of a single guy, Brooke realizing that the majority of her very formal style was best left in Chicago, and one week to go before the date of the move, I offered to help them settle into their new place. On the off chance that you haven't picked up on this yet, I am notorious for my quick decision-making. Remember that famous "I know it when I see it" quote from the Supreme Court? True, Justice Potter Stewart was referring to pornography, while I'm thinking more in terms of the perfect sofa, but you get the idea. Years of experience have taught me when a piece will work in a person's home and when it won't. I know when the price is right and when it's ridiculous. I know when something is too subdued, too loud, too stern, too frivolous, too sleek, too slouchy, too delicate, too heavy. I know when something is fantastic but still completely wrong for a particular personality, and I know when it's exactly right.

Brooke has never met a big decision that she didn't want to mull over. She is methodical, deliberate, and contemplative. But I've always felt that there's a time to let things happen and a time to make things happen, and I've logged in enough shopping hours with Brooke to know just how hard I can push my friend when it comes to making a purchase.

The Lower East Side vintage store I took Brooke to was filled with mid-century modern furniture that was affordable and chic. We found a 1960s sofa, a glass coffee table with a driftwood base, and an industrial lamp that could be clipped to a great glass-and-chrome desk. The pieces were both classic and contemporary, so when I convinced the shop's owner to do the impossible and deliver all the furniture to the new apartment that same day, despite the rain, I was ecstatic . . . and that made one of us.

Brooke was as close to a panic attack as anybody I've ever seen. "I just can't commit to this many things at once," she said, through her tears. I tried logic: "But today is the day we put aside to get all of the main things for your living room, and look how lucky we are to find so many wonderful things, all in one spot!" When that didn't dry her eyes, I tried economics: "Listen, I know the value of these things, and I'm telling you, you're getting a terrific deal!" Strike two.

Finally, I tried Michael. He was in Europe on business at the time, so we began sending photos of each piece for his review and input.

Everything was delivered that same afternoon.

The desk now sits in front of a large casement window that fills the room with light and charm. It's not unusual to find a pile of papers on that desk marked "Do Not Move," because if Michael doesn't make it absolutely clear, Brooke tends to straighten up in a way that drives him a little nuts. She used to smooth out all his crumpled receipts and place them in a pretty box, but she's learning to take a more hands-off approach. Michael's notebooks, a few pieces of mail, family snapshots, and a ceramic typewriter that holds his Post-it notes and paper clips all have a place on his side of the desk. There's also a rusted old spike from the railroad yards in McCook, Nebraska, a town comprising of 5.4 square miles in Red Willow County, where Michael's grandfather worked switching engines on the freight trains. And there's something else on the desk: a letter opener, its black-and-red painted handle carved into the shape of a spade, a diamond, a club, and a heart. Michael's father whittled it as a boy, but that Nebraska kid couldn't have known the letter opener would one day sit on his son's desk in New York City. Bob Hainey died when he was 35 years old and Michael was only 6. Michael has written a riveting account of his father's life and the mysterious circumstances of his death, titled *After Visiting Friends*.

With the exception of a framed invitation to Michael's first gallery show, and some very cool boxes where Brooke tucks away her work, there is nothing extraneous on her side of the desk. At night they sit across from each other, Michael in his squishy chrome-and-caramel leather chair—it's Italian and part of a pair he's had for years—Brooke in her high-back black patent-leather chair—it's French and part of a set she's had for years—with their laptops touching: the perfect definition of modern love.

The rest of Brooke and Michael's home is a tribute to couplehood. The art and photography books belong to Michael, the fashion books are Brooke's. The sophisticated, moody colors that percolate through the apartment are a little of each of them. The black leather medicine ball by the coffee table is Michael's but it's pretty sturdy and, believe it or not, Brooke likes to perch on it whenever they're in need of extra seating. The crow paintings above their sofa, striking yet restrained, were painted by Michael. "The black crow was the first real birthday present I ever gave Brooke," he told me. "I'd been lusting after it for a while, and

it's still the best birthday present I've ever received," Brooke added. She's not the only gift recipient. Michael gave me one of the paintings from his crow series as a housewarming gift and it's now hanging in my library. See that chair with the Greek-key cut-velvet pillow on it? The chair was Michael's, the pillow was Brooke's. Next to it is an Italian lamp from the 1960s that they bought together. The bowl of bocce balls with a vintage airplane thrown in for good measure is his. The luminous blown-glass shells from Murano on the antique tray are hers, and by laying them next to two small sculptures of slightly beat-up-looking heads that Michael found at a flea market, they're creating a perfect combo platter of refined and rustic.

The chrome bookcase also comes from our first shopping day, but the rock crystal tree covered in sparkly silver-and-white-agate leaves that sits on one of its shelves comes from Brooke. Actually, that tree was originally mine. I had it in Chicago, but Brooke always adored it, so one Christmas I wrapped it up and gave it to her. For a second she couldn't imagine how I could ever part with something she considered so special—unless there was actually something wrong with the thing. "Is it broken?" she asked, turning it over and over, in search of the problem. I had to explain that it wasn't broken, it was just beautiful and I wanted her to have it. So Brooke got a twinkly tree and I got the right to tease her about it for the next fifty years.

The other really amazing thing in that bookcase is the doodle a colleague of Michael's did as they sat through an awards dinner that seemed to be droning on forever. As portraits go, it doesn't really rank right up there with the *Mona Lisa*, but I found a little red frame for it because the artist did manage to say something about Michael's wit and style . . . or maybe just the fact that he hung on to the tiny line drawing says it all.

But the one item that stopped me in my tracks the first time I saw it, the thing that I think says the most about Michael, is a single sentence scribbled in pencil on a slightly stained scrap of paper: "Michael, be careful when using electric drill. Gramp." The note is framed and hanging in Brooke and Michael's entryway. "I had just left Chicago and moved to New York and I couldn't afford a bed, so I decided to build one myself," he told me. "My grandfather was a very fine craftsman with a well-stocked tool bench. He put together a care package of screwdrivers, a hammer, and an electric drill, and he mailed it to me, along with this note." It seems that Michael's grandfather was a man of few words, but I love that Michael knew not to throw those words away—in fact, he framed them. Who would think to do that? A writer, that's who!

The entry is filled with Michael's work in vintage frames, including a simple oil on canvas of a woman with her face blacked out. "I wanted to do a series about absence," Michael explained. "I like that she still has a personality, she still makes you feel something." He's right, the faceless portrait is mesmerizing. The brown velvet bench with gilded legs is nineteenth century French. Brooke brought it from her old life, along with the blown-glass raindrop chandelier. That chandelier is one of the first vintage pieces Brooke and I ever bought together. To me, the chandelier and the vintage Louis Vuitton suitcases sitting under the bench, and all of the old frames, battered bowls, and silver vases represent the weekends we spent laughing and talking and foraging through hundreds of little dives and tag sales and antiques malls north of Chicago. I look up at those blue raindrops and see the start of our twenty-year shopping spree.

The painting of the lady in the periwinkle party dress who looks like she could benefit from a few milligrams of Lexapro was a gift from Brooke's step-grandmother. I love that picture and I bet Don Draper would love it, too. The French chair beneath the lady in blue also comes from Brooke's old life—she found it online and we reupholstered it together. The chair is romantic and regal and, when paired with a charcoal-gray pinstripe pillow, sends a clear message that this couple has a well-defined sense of irony. Next to the chair is a vintage Italian cube from the '70s—a chic leftover from Michael's life before there was a Brooke in it, as well as a good place to hold another collection of art books, this one topped with a weathered old starfish.

Brooke doesn't depend on a cube or even the floor to hold her collection of shoes. One day she walked into a store and fell in love with a French, silk-lined curio cabinet and bought it on the spot. I loved it, too, and then something dawned on me: "You don't have to use your cabinet to hold porcelain figures," I told her. "Why not put your favorite shoes inside?" Brooke had the peeling paint refinished, some extra shelves added, and moved the piece right into her bedroom, where it now stores forty pairs of her favorite shoes and provides her a lot of pleasure, not to mention extra closet space.

This is a couple who are not only madly in love but also have wild respect for each other. Brooke leaves Michael tender Post-it notes, Michael brings Brooke her morning coffee, and together they've learned how to be married to each other. He let go of some closet space because Brooke is worth jamming a few jackets into the kitchen pantry for. And she let go of the need for perfection, because she realized that life is inherently messy and because Michael's happiness is more important than a few wadded-up receipts on a desk—and because it turns out that sitting on a dilapidated leather medicine ball is surprisingly comfortable for her.

I can't say it enough: The correct order for achieving joy is people, then animals, then things. Sooner or later most of us realize we can't change the other person, and we really don't even want to. We make concessions and compromises and come to understand that their way has its logic, and so does ours. It's what I call "imperfectly perfect." And that's the aesthetic that moves me the most about Brooke and Michael.

The truth is, their stuff probably shouldn't work together, but it does. Sometimes breaking the rules of design is what it takes to tell the story of who two people are when they're together. And reimagining your style to make room for who your partner is results in an interior that, like most great love affairs, is, and will forever be, perfectly imperfect.

SOONER OR LATER MOST OF US REALIZE
WE CAN'T CHANGE THE OTHER PERSON,
AND WE REALLY DON'T EVEN WANT TO.

NATE BERKUS

I'VE ALWAYS BEEN DRAWN TO THE ENERGY of New York City—the people let you know exactly where you stand within seconds of saying hello, you're never more than a twenty-two-minute subway ride from dim sum or tapas, on any given day in Central Park you'll find an old guy playing tenor sax or a rescue dog learning to walk on a leash, and you'll spot a battered copy of the book you've been searching high and low for being sold on the sidewalk in front of Zabar's. As a kid I watched movies like *Arthur* and *Working Girl* and *The First Wives Club,* and I thought New York was glamorous and gritty and mesmerizing and magic in a way I'd never seen before—a place where anything was possible. On most days I still feel that way.

I moved to Manhattan in baby steps. I had spent so much time visiting Fernando, and developing a steady stream of business in the city, that by the summer of 2006, with one foot still firmly planted in Chicago, I finally decided to actually buy a tiny, prewar 550-square-foot West Village apartment, a brand-new toothbrush, and a MetroCard. Chicago still felt like home, but Manhattan felt like it was at least worth a try.

By 2011, I was as ready as I was ever going to be to make a permanent move. My company was well established, and my staff was strong enough to take on the challenge of running the business without needing my physical presence on a daily basis. We were working with clients from coast to coast, which meant that when I wasn't boarding a plane to fly cross-country for another *Oprah* makeover show, I was hopping a flight to Florida, the Hamptons, Southern California—you name it. The truth was, Chicago is where I started. I didn't really *need* to be there anymore, so when I was offered the opportunity to launch my talk show out of New York, it was as though the fates had given me the go-ahead to kick off the next chapter of my life.

A few years after settling full-time into my tiny West Village apartment, mutual friends introduced me to an architect named Carlos. He was whip-smart, genuinely thoughtful, tremendously talented, roughly the same height as me, and Jewish. That, my friends, is about as rare as finding a unicorn under your bathroom sink.

I think all of us absorb lessons from the people in our lives, old or young, friends or lovers, parents or children. Carlos was born and raised in Mexico City. His references were so different from mine that I didn't know what to expect when it came time to actually see his apartment. What if he secretly collected thousands of those little Sweet 'n Low packets or celebrity hair or something? *Please, if nothing else,* I prayed, *let the place be clean.* I'm happy to say that his home was not only immaculate, there wasn't a bad oil painting in sight. It wasn't long before we fell in love.

In the months leading up to the launch of my talk show, Carlos and I rented a modern, white box created by renowned French architect Jean Nouvel. The apartment was, and is, a minor miracle of design. I always thought there was something to be said for living in an aerie overlooking the Hudson River, and here it is: sleek lines, white walls, and polished concrete countertops. The view was riveting—*Arthur, Working Girl,* and *The First Wives Club* all rolled into one! Everything was state-of-the-art. The sinks and the cabinetry were flawless. The glass-front refrigerator couldn't have been better for a guy who likes to decant his eggs. Look, I don't care how many times you reread that sentence, it's still going to say that I decant my eggs. (I cut the expiration date off the carton, set it at the bottom of a plain glass bowl, and place the eggs on top.)

Moving on.

I loved the juxtaposition of my vintage things sitting in an unmarred modern space. I loved the sunlight and how it made all our stuff pop; almost the way a sterile white backdrop in a photo studio allows you to see everything a little bit better. I loved being able to go running along the river all the way to Wall Street and back. I loved having an open space where we could easily entertain. The first things I bought for the apartment were thirty champagne glasses, so mimosas could happen on the spot. Carlos would make the waffles, I'd pour the orange juice, and together we would have fifteen friends over for a spur-of-the-moment Sunday brunch. I loved decorating with pieces we had found together in Mexican vintage shops, things that represented both of us, mixed in with objects and furniture from my tiny West Village flat, and books and lighting fixtures from Carlos's old place. And believe me, it was not lost on either of us that two grandchildren of immigrants could sit and have our morning coffee while staring at the Statue of Liberty. The apartment was cinematic and chic, pristine and perfect; it was the American dream come true. There was only one small problem—it was completely wrong for me.

Living up in the sky with floor-to-ceiling windows made me feel unmoored. I had already experienced the sensation of the earth opening up, and it left me vulnerable in ways I hadn't really counted on. I wasn't exactly miserable; I didn't have vertigo or anything. I was just kind of disoriented and . . . floaty. It felt like I was living on a theme-park ride and I wanted off.

For better or for worse, we are heavily influenced by the places where we've lived as children. I've lived in traditional houses my whole life. Give me something cracked or banged up, give me tarnished brass or mottled brick, the height of a baseboard, the profile of a molding, and I'm home. It turns out I'm not a big fan of asymmetry and interesting angles; I like my rooms square. I like stone fireplaces and ancient grout and knots in the hardwood floors. I like knowing that somebody else has lived in a place before me. They say that life isn't about learning new lessons so much as learning the same old ones again and again; if this apartment did nothing else for me, it reinforced that I want hardware that's been touched by many hands.

I need to live in a more familiar, storied way, surrounded by stuff that has age and patina and tales to tell.

Hosting your own show isn't exactly as brutal as mining for coal, but it does require a staggering amount of hard work that has to come across as effortless on-screen. Taping six shows a week takes a toll both emotionally and physically. I was getting ready for the launch and simultaneously doing dozens of makeovers all across the country, which made it even more anxiety-provoking when I'd walk through the door at the end of the day into a space that just didn't feel right.

The irony wasn't lost on me: Here I was bounding onstage each morning, showing the audience how they could make their own spaces feel more like home, and not feeling even remotely at ease in my own place. One day, Carlos and I had a heart-to-heart. I told him I felt like we were living on a shelf inside of a really, really modern medicine cabinet. I told him I felt like one of the Hollywood Squares (Paul Lynde to block). I told him that this place just wasn't home. And he told me that he understood. I know, I know: A normal person would have poured a glass of tequila, put his feet up, and reminded himself that he was living there only temporarily, and that when the demands of producing and hosting a daily TV talk show cooled down, he could begin looking for a more traditional home. . . .

Normal has never been high on my priority list (Hello, my name is Nate, and I'm an egg decanter). Instead of the feet on the coffee table and the glass of tequila, I'd get home from a day of taping and immediately start trolling online real estate websites. Rather than asking Carlos how his day had gone (he'd recently launched his own fragrance line), I'd say, "Hey—check out this three-bedroom floor-through . . . do you think this could work for us?"

We looked at a lot of apartments over the next few months. We met broker after broker. We traipsed through hallways, peered into closets, tested water pressure, studied views, and said, "Thanks, we'll let you know," more times than I can tell you. Ideally, our next home would be in a charming neighborhood, where I could find a decent slice of pizza and a basic supermarket (I actually need laundry detergent more than smoked eel fillets) within walking distance. The space would have great bones, and I could renovate it using all the materials I love, like white-oak, hand-planed herringbone floorboards, marble mantels, iron-and-glass windows. I wanted a space that would showcase all the hardware I'd hunted down online or found in architectural salvage places. When all was said and done, I wanted some history.

When I walked into the apartment I finally ended up buying, it felt strangely familiar—I even wondered if maybe I'd once been to a party there. It took no more than a couple of seconds to realize that this was a space where I could be happy. For one thing, the apartment had two floors, a formal dining room, a space off the master bedroom that I knew we could transform into a great dressing room, a big, light-filled guest room with a terrace, and a family room that was big enough to fit a pair of floor-to-ceiling bookcases. But a space is only as good as what you put in it and I knew that almost every object and piece of furniture I owned would look beautiful here. There was nothing to think about—I made an offer on the spot, and it was accepted that afternoon.

Carlos was just as excited as I was. We started going back and forth to the new place, every six seconds, 'round the clock: *Should the dining room go here or there? What color do we paint the kitchen? Can we get away with leaving the bathroom tile alone?* And the biggest question: *How are we ever going to get this together with my work schedule?* From time to time, we all wonder who's really in charge of the world. My proof God exists is that I was able to arrange for this renovation to take place over the summer, so that by the time the show began taping again in late August, we'd be living in our new place. Unfortunately, before we could live, we had to move.

On a scale of things that make me want to curl into a ball and hyperventilate, moving falls just below an emergency appendectomy. At its best, the process is emotional and grueling; at its worst, it's traumatic and back-breaking. There's something about packing your life into boxes labeled "dining room," "bedroom," "miscellaneous," and then watching everything you own get shoved into the back of a stranger's truck that I just find harrowing. For one thing, I have never, ever moved on a sunny day. There's always a torrential thunderstorm. For another, I can't seem to relax until every last spoon is washed and in the drawer, every picture is hung, every sneaker has found a proper home in the closet.

If you were to add up all of the time I logged sleeping that first week after the move, it would come to approximately fifteen minutes—and I swear I was up twice during that quarter of an hour. Some people have nightmares about roller coasters raging out of control or walking naked across a college quad. Not me. I would wake up in the middle of the night and wonder, *Where is that silver dresser I bought online going to fit?* As soon as my bloodshot eyes flipped open in the morning, I sprang out of bed and went right back to staring down the cardboard boxes. And Carlos was with me every step of the way, measuring, hammering, and bandaging my toe each time I dropped something heavy on it. (For those of you playing the home game, that would be three times in a single afternoon.)

When I'm decorating a new space, my eye goes to every detail in a room simultaneously. I can't focus on any one thing. I need to understand the relationship of a table to everything that surrounds it. To me, the mathematical problem of creating a home is: How do I fit what is important to me in this new environment, and then add to those things in a way that makes them look correct and beautiful to my eye? Always, always the architecture—the size and scale of the room—dictates what works and what doesn't. I knew I needed four things: height, light, space, and character. When I walked into the apartment that would become our new home, the first things I noticed were the ten-and-a-half-foot ceilings. Next I looked at the distribution of the rooms—how a chain of rooms open into each other. I looked to see where the sunlight was. I asked myself which rooms I'd want to spend the most time in. For example, the previous owners had a dining room that I decided to turn into my family room because my morning ritual is to have coffee and blueberries in front of the TV, and that room got the most light. I wanted rooms that would meet our needs. I didn't want a room that you just walked past unless you decided to throw a dinner party every couple of months. I wanted a place where you could set up your laptop and stretch out with your papers, where you could have a business meeting *or* have a few friends over for take-out Thai food. The universal question that people have to ask themselves is this: When I come home after a long day, do I have a soft place to land?

That's easy for me to say, right? The truth is, figuring out which things belong where, and what you really need to be comfortable and happy can be complicated. For what it's worth, I've been a professional decorator since 1996, but I still don't feel as confident in my own home as I do in other people's (it's kind of like the chef who makes himself peanut butter and jelly for dinner or the manicurist with ragged cuticles). I know when something looks right, but I also like standing in front of a piece of furniture and asking, "Do you like this?" and "Do you think this would work?" Left to my own devices, I will always bring in as many opinions as possible, so it only makes sense to me to have the opinion of the person I love. As far as I'm concerned, the pursuit of love is tied up with the desire to live beautifully, and I count myself lucky to live with a partner whose taste I trust and whose opinion I value and who is not, thank God, as much of a maniac as I am. Carlos once told a mutual friend, "When Nate goes silent I know I'll be carrying a chair." There aren't a whole lot of people who are willing to haul a silver dresser into three different rooms with me, but when I find one, I'm extremely grateful.

So what's the difference between doing a makeover and decorating your own home? Well, at heart, a TV or magazine makeover is almost the opposite of creating a home for yourself. Actually it isn't about creating a home so much as expediting the process. Every single makeover begins with the following questions: *What is the look and the feeling we're after? What is the color scheme? Where can we get the sofa?* I'm always asking myself, *What kind of information can I put into a makeover that people will learn from?* My job is to inspire others, while teaching them not to be intimidated. In real life, I'm the one who is forever seeking inspiration.

ONE DAY, I LOOKED AROUND AND REALIZED THAT I WAS HOME.

And I find it everywhere. I'm inspired by people who seem to be juggling a thousand different things, all at the same time. And I'm especially moved by those who are capable of having a good laugh when a couple of those thousand things end up getting away from them. I'm inspired by people who've got phenomenal street style, because they're fearless; they'll mix patterns or eras or textures in such an interesting, carefree, witty way that you feel like you're being moved forward by unseen forces. I'm inspired by the young, the risk-takers, the people who establish the rules, and the people who are willing to break them. And I've always admired that European thing, where a person will buy just one outfit, but that outfit is tailored to perfection from beautiful fabric, and they find a million different ways to wear it. I've yet to be able to pull it off personally, but I'm profoundly inspired by true minimalists, because they're always so fiercely protective of the quality of the things they surround themselves with.

So, as you can see, for me inspiring others and being inspired are two separate issues. My job as a decorator is being able to distill the essence of people from their words, and tell their stories through objects and color and fabric and furniture.

Including my own story. Because one day, I looked around and realized that I was home.

That realization was a quiet thing—music didn't swell as I came down a staircase bathed in a halo of golden light. No, I knew I was finally home when I reached for a screwdriver and realized that I didn't have to think about which cupboard it was stashed in. My muscle memory was finally activated. At last I knew what was inside each and every cabinet, drawer, and shelf, whether it was plates, cups, T-shirts, sneakers, or gift-wrapping (yes, I have a gift-wrap drawer, and that's all we're going to say about that).

My space reflects the life I've lived so far, and it's filled with stuff that has been with me for years, stuff that reminds me of where I've traveled, who I've loved, and where I want to go next. In my family room are gifts from friends; one gave me a Fornasetti plate for my fortieth birthday, and another pal gave me a Bottega Veneta picture frame. Corin Nelson, whom you read about a few chapters back, gave me a spectacular chunk of malachite that I keep on a stack of books. There's a vintage Louis Vuitton leather case I found at a flea market in Paris years ago; two funny brass puzzles I bought at a Japanese store on Melrose Avenue; an old Hermès picture frame, also from Paris; a pair of standing graphite feet that I gave to Carlos as a gift; and a lamp that used to sit on the desk a couple of apartments ago.

There was also some stuff I wasn't able to fit in my new space that's now resting comfortably in storage. In my Chicago apartment, I had a kitchen table and chairs that I still miss a lot. (I used to sit there and pick at the top, talking with friends for hours on end, so I was intimately acquainted with all the marks in the wood.) But I also did some recycling. The curtain panels are from my Chicago apartment. I found them years ago in a catalog and added some length to make them work in this space.

Those old iron bookshelves were salvaged from a Parisian bank. They come in a million pieces, so if you move them, you first have to take them apart and then reassemble them. They're so heavy they have to be bolted to the wall. It's really a lot of work, and really worth it. On top of one is an old brass clip lamp from my Chicago days that probably cost me all of $1.85.

The family room is my favorite room, the one I think is the most successful. I not only love what's *in* this room and how the objects stand out, I love what is *not* here, too. I think of the family room as an assortment of small beats—or moments—of color: a bright yellow tortilla holder from Mexico, and a scattering of woolen place mats I brought back from Thailand. Deborah Colman and Neil Kraus, two genius connoisseurs of decorative art and furniture who have influenced me greatly for as long as I've been a decorator, own one of my favorite shops, called Pavilion 20th Century. Over the years I've known them, the store has passed through more than a few incarnations. Deborah and Neil alter the design and the feeling of the interior over and over again. Many of my favorite things in the world, including those Parisian bookshelves, came from Pavilion.

It's easier to tell what a room has than what it lacks. So, quick: If I asked you for the defining characteristic of the family room, what would you say? It's this: With the exception of a table I bought especially for this place, there's nothing new in here.

The room had been painted white, and we kept it that way. I had the choice of placing grilles over the radiator and air conditioner, but that was just too much metal.

I painted the window frames black. The brass chairs—Fernando and I bought them together—came from my apartment in Chicago. I designed the pillows. The wicker table used to be in my Chicago bedroom, and the silver dresser from the 1970s (you may recall we lugged it to several different spots) I bought online for that modern, white apartment in New York. The black mirror is another Pavilion piece—it used to hang in my entry—and we found the majolica bust of Julius Caesar in an antiques store in Stamford, Connecticut.

The chair is one of a pair (and sharp-eyed readers will recognize the other in Brooke Cundiff and Michael Hainey's living room). That pillow on the chair is covered in a nineteenth-century Native American wool rug. The three photographs on the wall were a gift from Chicago photographer Doug Fogelson. Above the couch hangs one of my favorite pieces of art—I bought it with Carlos on my first trip to Mexico City. It's called *The Last Ranchero*.

The tiny coat that hangs in my stairwell belonged to my grandfather, and I can remember seeing pictures of him wearing it when he was a little boy. I had it in my first apartment in Chicago, in my final apartment in Chicago, and now I pass it dozens of times a day as I go up and down the stairs. It not only connects me to where I came from, but, like the man himself, it's just got a certain charm.

The story goes that my grandfather met my grandmother when he was the water sports director at Camp Pinemere in the Poconos and she showed up with three trunks' worth of wardrobe changes. He was a suit salesman who moved his family from the East Coast to the Midwest because that was his territory. He's 90 now, but to this day he can still rock loafers without socks, perfectly pressed khakis, a button-down Oxford shirt, a braided belt, and a navy blazer with brass buttons like nobody else. Also, like nobody else, he doesn't hesitate to call after catching a TV appearance to let me know that a shave wouldn't exactly kill me, or that I'd seem a lot more credible with a tie and a pocket square.

One of the questions I asked myself when I first saw the dining room was, *Is there enough space in here for floor-to-ceiling bookshelves?* My dream was to have all my books in a single spot, so Carlos got to work and, using his background as an architect, he was able to design it down to the millimeter. It's inspired by the second floor of Pierre Bergé's apartment in Paris. Jacques Grange was Bergé's decorator, and he's one of my design heroes. His first floor is very formal, but the second floor, where his office and bedroom and library are, has a slightly rustic, more casual quality. What we wanted to take from Bergé's place is the timeless feeling his home conveys. I think that's the thing everybody should consider before writing a check to a contractor: *Will this stand the test of time?* You have to just be in a room for a while, block out all the white noise, and honestly ask yourself, *Is this the hottest trend, the flavor of the month, or is this the navy blue blazer with brass buttons?* My grandfather taught me well: I go for the blue blazer every time. I walk into my dining room/library and I know that I will never tire of the waxed-wood planks in a chevron pattern on the floor because it's historic and never goes out of style. Nobody will take a chisel to my marble fireplace because after a few years I decide I want wood instead. The marble fireplace is a nineteenth-century classic. And I know that I'll always take pleasure in these simple bookcases—they still work for Pierre Bergé and years from now they'll still work for me, too.

The books on display here are a combination of mine, Fernando's, and Carlos's. They all revolve around the same subjects: architecture, design, travel, jewelry, fashion, photography, furniture, paintings, drawings, and museum collections. None are there for show. Some I use for inspiration, others I reference when I'm working for clients, and still others just make me smile.

When Fernando died, I took almost all his books and lots of small objects, though nothing of any real monetary value. The watches and the cuff links he loved went to his nephews, but when he and I first began spending time together, Fernando would hand me books that he'd marked up with little Post-it notes because he wanted to show me something: a thought-provoking quote, an amazing face, maybe just a place he wanted us to see together someday. I've always believed that there is something extraordinary and very circular about opening a book that once really mattered to someone I love, and I still take comfort in being able to touch something that he touched. Now a part of what Fernando collected and cherished is celebrated by the way I live.

The two pictures are by the German artist Günther Förg—they were the first grown-up art I ever bought. I always hear about people being intimidated by the art world—it can feel so clubby, so insular. But I was never impressed by names, because I saw virtually every major name come through the auction house where I worked and it taught me that the true value of a piece is always determined by the market. When you put something up on the block, you find out very quickly what people think it's worth. I've had more than one client ask me if a piece is good, but really, the only question you have to ask when you're buying art is, *Do I like it?* If you like it, then yes, it's good.

The dining table was my conference table in the Chicago office, and I salvaged the

THE ONE QUESTION YOU HAVE TO ASK WHEN YOU'RE BUYING ART IS, DO I LIKE IT? IF YOU LIKE IT, THEN YES, IT'S GOOD.

1950s-era chairs, with their original upholstery, paint, and nail heads intact, from a client. They were made by the French company Jansen. Jacqueline Kennedy used Jansen when she redecorated the White House, and the Duchess of Windsor used Jansen for her home outside of Paris, so I guess I'm in pretty good company. The woven Belgian wallpaper I found at Lowe's.

You can see in the custom iron-and-glass doors the influence my time spent living in France has had. I love the idea of metal interior doors. Unfortunately, when they were first installed, the workers used white caulk to hold the panes of glass in place and I was less than happy with the results. I insisted they replace it with black putty.

The dining table is more of a working table than a place to eat (I usually have dinner on the couch in the family room). Books sit there, mostly volumes I'm referencing for various design projects. I brought the beaded hat home from South Africa. That hand was created by the artist Pedro Friedeberg. I actually paid a visit to his home in Mexico City, and as the night went on, and more and more tequila was consumed, I finally found the nerve to slur, "Would you be offended if I wanted to buy something here?" And without missing a beat, he answered, "I would be offended if you didn't."

Also in the dining room are a few things I have had with me forever. The pottery fish candleholders belonged to Fernando (I always picture the way he'd set the table with them) and so did the Chinese silver compote and the papier-mâché lacquer vase. Carlos and I bought the Napoleon plates at a Florida antiques mall. I came across the little set of dishes and the wine pourer in Chicago years ago. The runner is from Thailand. There's also a book about Patmos, one of my favorite places to go when I need to change my scene and catch up with the friends I've made there over the years.

In the kitchen, I painted the cabinets, and replaced the existing backsplash with plain subway tile. For the island, I wanted something that felt like it had always been there, and I found just the thing from a Chicago antiques dealer. The fact that it's on casters, and has two shelves where I can put my serving pieces, is great, and I could not love the stone top more.

The leather screen in my bedroom comes from my Chicago apartment, and the bed has an upholstered headboard I designed that I had slipcovered in cotton velvet with leather welting. The nightstands are from the sixties, made out of lacquered goatskin by Italian furniture designer Aldo Tura. I found the bronze-lacquer-and-leather desk in Mexico City. The lamps have Italian eighteenth-century bases, and the shades are made of old grasscloth. The folk art piece is from my old bedroom in Chicago; it's some kind of scorecard, sketched onto black linen. The cashmere pillow and the pillow with

braided leather cording sit beside a $9 Mexican embroidered pillow and a cashmere blanket that practically weighs as much as I do.

My closet is a total fantasy. Carlos literally sketched out the space, which the contractors then mocked up. The closet was brought in piece by piece, like LEGOs. Every shelf is beveled. The ottoman is from my library in Chicago, and the carpet Carlos and I picked out together. The light fixture is American 1960s, and used to hang in my Chicago guest room. The millwork is French Directoire–inspired and painted pale gray, with unlacquered brass hardware and inset mirrors.

The mirrors in the bathroom come from my master bathroom in Chicago. As for the stuffed leather rhinoceros head hanging on the wall, he was a wedding present to my parents, from Abercrombie & Fitch, in the days when Abercrombie was a hunting and fishing store, and he lives with me wherever I go. The bust is of Shakespeare, while the lighting Carlos and I ordered from Nantucket. A picture that Fernando took of birds at night hangs above an old French 1950s shelf, which holds towels from my own collection. The matchbook engraved with a "B" was a gift from my friend Barri Leiner, who you met in chapter 4. The horn cup I brought home from Asia.

As I mentioned, my mother and I both gravitate toward stone and fossils and dendrites—they're one of the few presents she knows are safe to surprise me with. But this particular star sapphire and dendrite my friend Ahmad and I found in Tucson, Arizona.

I swiped the marble fireplace from my master bedroom in Chicago, and reinstalled it here in the guest room. The old French urn on the wood vase is from my Chicago entry. The chair in the corner is a prototype for Niedermaier, while the lamp is 1960s-era. On the side table is a brass lamp, the baskets are Mexican, the horn tray comes from Sri Lanka, and the two candlesticks belonged to Fernando.

I have to say, it was fun to position the nineteenth-century French fireplace across from a nineteenth-century French side table in the living room. I reupholstered the benches in corduroy; the coffee table used to be a bench, but I replaced the top with a piece of old Belgian limestone. I have had the little brown chair for twenty years, upholstered in cashmere. The funny little sculpture I bought at an art fair in Venice. The seagrass rug comes from a catalog.

I wanted to begin collecting English Regency mahogany furniture, which is why I bought the center table. (A good rule of thumb is that when the trend moves away from collecting something, it's the perfect time to buy it, and right now English antiques are a great value.) One of the first chairs I ever owned was the pony chair with the black cotton velvet seat. I remember scrounging my money together to buy it from the auction house I worked for in Chicago when I was 23.

On the side table is a collection of some of my favorite things of all time: a Belgian pottery vase; an Alexander Noll bowl carved from a solid piece of ebony; a bronze

paperweight I bought from a jeweler in Naples; a C. Jeré sculpture; and another series of crystals that were a gift from my mom. The French chairs, which I found in a Sag Harbor antiques store, are probably the most valuable pieces in the house. They were created by one of the most talented and refined mid-century designers who ever lived, Gilbert Poillerat. His work is featured in the Museum of Decorative Arts in the Louvre.

This 1970s-era chrome-and-carved-wood French cabinet comes from my apartment in Chicago. Michael Hainey did the bird painting (you may recognize a similar one in Michael and Brooke's home) and gave it to me as a housewarming present. It's one of my favorite pieces, which makes a lot of sense, given that he's one of my favorite people. I bought the 1950s-era wood-carved shell in Paris, and it sits beside a Marina Karella sculpture. Colors come in and out of vogue every season, but black and white never get old. On the wall is a collection of vintage black-and-white Fornasetti plates. Fornasseti is one of those rule breakers I was thinking of when I was telling you about people who inspire me. His point of view was strong and his patterns were wild and whimsical and absolutely unique.

The doorknob is French vintage, circa 1970.

This hat belonged to Fernando, and so did the Chinese vase, the cloche, and the skull. The bracelets I brought back from South Africa after visiting the Oprah Leadership Academy for Girls. The horse was one of a pair of Fernando's, and the belt I brought home from Peru. There is a vintage Hermes toiletry kit from the 1930s that I found years ago at a flea market in Paris. The chest of drawers comes from a roadside antiques shop in rural Michigan. They're very rural in sensibility but also very refined. The original stamp is faded but still visible in the back of a drawer. It tells me that it was made in Belgium; how it found its way to a dusty little shop halfway between Chicago and Saugatuck will remain a mystery. The bird was a gift from my mother's wonderful friend Joyce Straus. Also, there are framed notes from various friends, mixed in with photographs of me with my niece and nephew. I'm a sucker for a fantastic piece of jewelry, and I keep that 1960s-era necklace on that book.

The bed comes from my Chicago apartment, and the lamp is leather, with an ostrich egg. The embroidered tapestry on the wall is traditional Mexican, and the bracket I have had forever. The mirror is 1960s-era Italian.

The powder room is decidedly masculine; I've always been very no-frills. I bought the leather sink and the sconces online. I had the mirror made from rope, and the towel bar is salvaged. The wallpaper is Fornasetti malachite, because every

man, woman, and child, blonde, brunette, and redhead looks amazing against that particular paper.

The lantern in the stairwell was the kitchen fixture in my Chicago apartment.

I am fully aware that I am fortunate to lead a beautiful life, that I have worked hard for it, and that it matters a lot to me. At the same time, in no way is my New York space *complete,* because the truth is, a space, or an individual room, is never really done. To me, decorating is the lifelong pursuit of what could be more interesting, more harmonious, better, what can be discovered, unearthed, combined. Some people sit in their family rooms at night rehashing their day or thinking about what's on TV. I sit in mine and wonder, *Would that wicker table look good in the bedroom? Should I put two more chairs here? Should this bookcase be moved two inches to the right? Why are there two chests of drawers in here?* It doesn't mean I'm always actively seeking something new, only that I'm open to change if and when it occurs to me.

The greatest evolution for me as a person over the years is the knowledge that situations change, nothing is ever perfect, and some stuff you just can't control. Today, I know that I can fix anything that's not working. In my early days as a

decorator, I was terrified to make a mistake, take a risk, spend someone else's money. But who wants their work to be based in fear? The bottom line is that there's always that moment when the eighteen-wheeler pulls up to the curb, and you've got to be ready to think on your feet. I've been doing this for so many years now that I no longer hesitate to say to a client, "Those two chairs we ordered for the living room would look better in the bedroom." It's gotten to a point where my team and I must have the flexibility to change our minds without the client peering over our shoulders. My knowledge and confidence comes from taking a sofa out of one room and putting it in another, by replacing an accent wall with a single unifying color, by incorporating depth by layering in family photos and flea market treasures—and making hundreds of rooms come to life as a result.

Surviving the tsunami helped give that priority shift a push. I used to stress out when a room wasn't perfect, or a piece of furniture showed up twenty-four hours late. These days, I shrug my shoulders. When you have lived through the worst thing you can imagine, it unlocks the shackles, creatively speaking. It sets you free. Time and experience and a few triumphs and, of course, my fair share of mistakes have shown me that there is no one right way to design a room.

SO HERE'S TO THE THINGS THAT
LIFT US UP, ANCHOR OUR LIVES—AND
TELL THE WORLD WHO WE ARE.

That's what I love about building a home for myself and what I love about building a home for other people. The recipe isn't all that complicated: You just have to add your life, your travels, your memories, the people you've loved, the people who've loved you back, all the stuff that's crossed your path along the way—and then mix.

At the end of the day, my attachment isn't to my new home—which is really just a series of rooms and walls—but to the things that fill it. Which is why I know that if for some reason I ever ended up living in a studio apartment again, I'd be happy. Because I would have only what I need. But in my case, as a lifelong aficionado of stuff, what I *need* is the exact same thing as what I *want*. So here's to the things that lift us up, anchor our lives—and tell the world who we are.

THINGS THAT MATTER TO . . .

BARBARA BERGER, 1
As an avid collector, I find it so hard to choose just a single piece, but this handbag represents my jewelry, toy, and handbag collection in one. I think it has a great sense of humor and beauty.

JULIANNE MOORE, 2
I love this lamp. It's a piece of sculpture, plaster, made in the 1970s, probably cast from the artist's own hands. I love a human, physical element in objects.

AHMAD SARDAR-AFKHAMI, 3
I love these monkeys. They're not the most precious or rare things that I have in my home . . . but I couldn't imagine morning coffee without their naughty gaze. They used to be in the bedroom but would get up to no good when I was asleep. After a long separation, they now live together on my dining room table. They were a rather surprising and delightful birthday present from a dear friend.

TALI MAGAL, 4
I found this "driftwood angel" while walking along the beach in Santa Teresa, Costa Rica, with my then-boyfriend-now-husband, back in 2003. She literally washed ashore right at our feet and stood there shining in the sun like a dancing angel. She has now lived with me in all my New York City apartments since I found her and is always displayed in a place of pride. Our angel serves to remind us of nature, the oceans, LOVE . . . and it makes me feel protected.

KATHRYN STOCKETT, 5
Sometimes it's who the gift is from, other times it's the gift itself that makes it so important to you. In this case, it was both. My favorite book in the world is *Lolita*. Amy Einhorn, my publisher, sent me this signed copy for my birthday. She searched and begged and haggled—I cried when I received it. It's not just RARE—it's pretty darn flammable. It's what I'd grab if the house was on fire.

P.S. I wonder what Nabokov's publisher gave him that he cherished?

MAYA ANGELOU, 6
These figures, in *The Passing of Sister Sookie* by Phoebe Beasley, resemble women in my grandmother's prayer meeting group. I have carried this painting all over the world and I hang it in a room where I spend most of my time. I was at 20th Century Fox as their first Black female writer/producer and I hung it on a wall opposite my desk. Wherever I am, anywhere in the world, and whenever I'm there, if I question the morality of a situation in which I find myself, I look at the painting and ask, "What would Momma do?" I can almost hear her say, "Now, Sister, you know right from wrong, do right, just do right."

CARLOS HUBER, 7
These books are important to me because they represent who and what I love. They were a gift from Nate from our first year together, and they are first-edition architecture books from 1738. The author, J. F. Blondel, was extremely influential in architectural history. To be able to appreciate the illustrations and read the texts MAKES ME SO HAPPY. I love these books, and books love you back. . . .

PAULA LEUTWYLER, 8
Even though I have traveled extensively throughout my life, nothing prepared me for the extraordinary city of Venice. The first time we visited, we were fortunate enough to stay at the Hotel Danieli. Again, I was ill-prepared for the opulence and beauty of everything around me. At the end of the trip, I wanted something to remind me of this place. I could not find anything—except the key to the room where we stayed; please don't tell anyone. . . .

DONNA BRAZILE, 9
The masks are from Africa. Bought them or brokered for them in several countries—South Africa, Namibia, Ghana, Egypt, Morocco, Kenya, Somalia, and Nigeria. They are my connection to my ancestral homeland. They bring to life what only spirit can show—warmth, compassion, and grace.

CHRISTINA SALWAY, 10
Our wedding cake topper is particularly meaningful to me and my husband, not only because it serves as a wonderful, everyday memento of our wedding, but also because it's such a perfect symbol of our life together—a little kooky, definitely romantic, and always uniquely ours. . . .

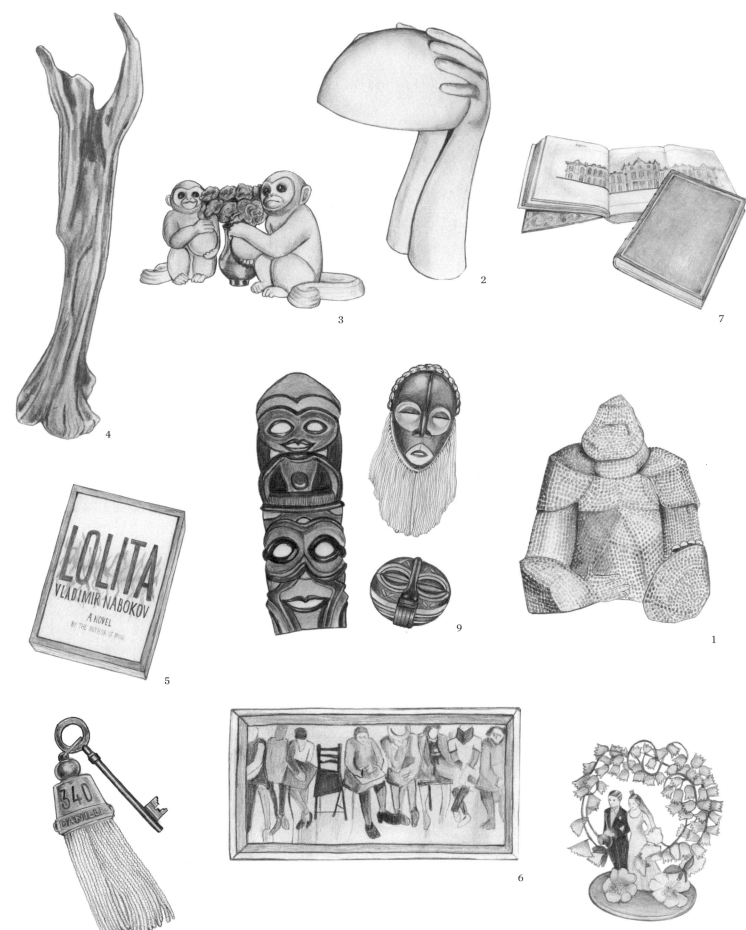

ACKNOWLEDGMENTS

This book—and, in fact, my life and joys as I know them—would not be possible without
the following exceedingly special, creative, warm, often hysterically funny people who have
mattered, and continue to matter, to me. I wish to thank:

My family, which keeps expanding, thanks to my two sisters-in-law, Yassi and Kelly. My niece Kate; her
brother, Chase; my niece Chloe; and the Goose, otherwise known as Caden, whose three-year-old voice
I hope against hope never changes.

To my siblings—Jesse, Steve, Marni, Dan, and Bob—you are all such an important part of
my life; I respect and admire the lives you have created for yourselves.

My parents, Nancy and Marshall Golden, and Michael and Sher Berkus.

Kristin Giese, whose leadership, creativity, thrifting skills, Dairy Queen radar, and guidance
have brought me to where I am, which happens to be exactly where I want to be.

The incredibly talented staff of Nate Berkus Inc., in both Chicago and NYC,
who continue to inspire me each day.

Holly Jacobs and the Too Live Crew at Sony Pictures Television.

All of my dear friends at Harpo.

Executive producer of spectacular birthday dinners, Nantucket holidays, casino security,
as well as TV shows, Corin Nelson.

Julie Grau and the team at Spiegel & Grau and Random House.

Richard Pine, Rich Heller, Richard Hoffstetter, for your solid advice 24/7, I thank you.

To all of you who agreed to be a part of this new sort of design book, I thank you for
allowing all of us into your homes and telling your stories.

Michael and Brooke Hainey, Carlos Huber, Brian Sawyer, Ahmad Sardar-Afkhami, Andre Viana,
Andre Mellone, Marjorie Gubelman, Alondra de la Parra, Princess Olga of Greece, Claudia Levy,
Jonathan Lelonek, Pierre-Henri Mattout, Barbara Marion Berger, the Soboroff family, the Stone sisters,
Steve Berg, Amanda McPhillips, Jason Kurtz, Kevin Boyer, the Bengoechea family,
Oprah Winfrey, Sheri Salata, Scott Seviour, Barri Leiner, and Rich Baretta.

To photographers Roger Davies, Rainer Hosch, and Kevin Trageser, as well as writer
Peter Smith and book designer Gabriele Wilson, you made this dream a reality.

And to Lisa Kogan, the sensitivity, grace, and vulnerability with which you captured my story
and the stories in this book have brought me to free-falling tears of gratitude on more than
one occasion. Thank you, friend with a magic pen.

MANY THANKS TO

LIST OF ILLUSTRATIONS

ABOUT THE AUTHOR

Nate Berkus is founder of the interior design firm Nate Berkus Associates. For two years he was the host of *The Nate Berkus Show*, an Emmy Award–winning, nationally syndicated daytime talk show. His work has appeared in *Elle Decor, O: The Oprah Magazine, InStyle, The New York Times, Vanity Fair*, and *House Beautiful*. He is the author of the *New York Times* bestseller *Home Rules*. He lives in New York City.

ABOUT THE PHOTOGRAPHER

Roger Davies arrived in New York at the age of 22, after studying photography and film in England. His work was taken him around the world and his photographs have graced the pages of *Architectural Digest, AD* (France), *Condé Nast Traveler, Harper's Bazaar UK*, and *Elle Decor*. He lives in Laurel Canyon, California, with his wife and son.